Our Ageing World

Editor

Craig Donnellan

First published by Independence
PO Box 295
Cambridge CB1 3XP
England

British Library Cataloguing in Publication Data
Our Ageing World – (Issues Series)
I. Donnellan, Craig II. Series
305.2'6

ISBN 1 86168 213 1

Printed in Great Britain
MWL Print Group Ltd

Typeset by
Claire Boyd

Cover
The illustration on the front cover is by
Pumpkin House.

CONTENTS

Chapter One: Ageing Trends

Chapter Two: Ageism in the Workplace

Chapter Three: Ageing and Health

Introduction

Our Ageing World is the sixteenth volume in the **Issues** series. The aim of this series is to offer up-to-date information about important issues in our world.

Our Ageing World examines the issue of ageing in society, in the workplace and in healthcare.

The information comes from a wide variety of sources and includes:
Government reports and statistics
Newspaper reports and features
Magazine articles and surveys
Literature from lobby groups
and charitable organisations.

It is hoped that, as you read about the many aspects of the issues explored in this book, you will critically evaluate the information presented. It is important that you decide whether you are being presented with facts or opinions. Does the writer give a biased or an unbiased report? If an opinion is being expressed, do you agree with the writer?

Our Ageing World offers a useful starting-point for those who need convenient access to information about the many issues involved. However, it is only a starting-point. At the back of the book is a list of organisations which you may want to contact for further information.

*****

Older people in the United Kingdom

Basics

In the United Kingdom, in 2000, there were over 10.7 million older people (10,789,000):

9,021,000 in England
924,000 in Scotland
586,000 in Wales
259,000 in Northern Ireland.

An ageing population

In 2000, the population of the United Kingdom based on mid-year estimates was 59,756,000. Of this figure, 18.1% were over pensionable age:

- 6,915,000 were women aged 60 and over (of whom 5,442,000 were aged 65 and over)
- 3,875,000 were men aged 65 and over
- 9,316,000 were people aged 65 and over
- 4,399,000 were people aged 75 and over
- 1,162,000 were people aged 85 and over.[1]

In 1998 a man of 60 could expect to live for another 19 years and a woman of the same age for 22.6 years.[2]

In 1996, in England and Wales, 5,523 people (4,943 women and 580 men) were aged 100 and over. In 2036 it is estimated that there will be 39,000 people in this age group, and, by 2066, 95,000.[3]

Looking at the ethnic minority population in Great Britain, in 1997/ 99, 7% of the population was aged 65 and over and belonging to a minority ethnic group. Within specific groups:

- 15% of Black-Caribbean people were aged over 65
- 3% of Black-African people were aged over 65
- 10% of Indian people were aged over 65
- 7% of Pakistani people were aged over 65

- 6% of Bangladeshi people were aged over 65
- 9% of Chinese people were aged over 65.[4]

An ageing population in the future

The number of people over pensionable age, taking account of the change in the women's retirement age, is projected to increase from 10.7 million in 1998 to 11.9 million in 2011, and will rise to 12.2 million by 2021.[5]

Employment

In 2000, there were 5.71 million people aged between 50 and the State Pension Age in employment. The employment rate for men between the ages of 50 and 64 was 68.7%, and for women between the ages of 50 and 59 was 63.5%. This compares to an employment rate for all people of working age of 74.6%.[6]

In Spring 2000, 7.6% of men aged 65 and over and 8.2% of women aged 60 and over were still in employment.[7]

Income

The basic pension from April 2001 to April 2002 is £72.50 for a single pensioner, and £115.90 for a couple (claiming on the husband's contributions) per week.

In 1999/2000 single pensioners received, on average, £149 net income per week. Pensioner couples received £281 per week on average during the same period.[8]

Older pensioner households have lower incomes. In 1999/2000 pensioner couples where the man was aged over 75 received £245 net income per week on average, compared with

£299 net income per week for those aged under 75.[8]

In 1999/2000, 70% of pensioner households depended on state benefits for at least 50% of their income.[9]

In August 2000, 1,638,000 people aged 60 or over (single people or couples) in Great Britain were receiving Income Support (Minimum Income Guarantee) because of their low income.[10]

The Department for Work and Pensions estimates that, in 1999/2000, between 22% and 36% of pensioners who were entitled to Income Support, between 7% and 15% who were entitled to Housing Benefit, and between 30% and 36% entitled to Council Tax Benefit, did not claim.[11]

Living alone

In 2000, in the 65-74 age group, 19% of men and 37% of women lived alone, and 33% of men and 60% of women aged 75 and over lived alone.[12]

In 2000, the likelihood of living alone increased with age, with 50% of those aged 75 and over living alone in Great Britain, compared with 12% of those aged 25-44.[13]

In 2000, of people aged 65 to 74/75 and over in Great Britain:
- 76%/61% of men were married
- 56%/27% of women were married
- 9%/29% of men were widowed
- 31%/61% of women were widowed.[14]

References

1 *Population Trends 105*, Autumn 2001, © Crown Copyright 2001, table 1.5 (Population: age and sex) and table 1.2 (Population: national).

2 Ibid., table 5.1 (Expectation of life [in years] at birth and selected age).

3 The demography of centenarians in England and Wales. *PT 96*, Summer 1999, © Crown Copyright 1999, annex 1.

4 The sizes and characteristics of the minority ethnic populations of Great Britain – latest estimates, *PT 105*, op. cit., table 3 (Population size, per cent distribution by age and median age by ethnic group, 1997-99, Great Britain).

5 *National population projections: 1998-based*, National Statistics, © Crown Copyright 2000, table 3.2 (Actual and projected population by age, UK, 1998-2021).

6 *Age discrimination in employment: seventh report . . . of the Education and Employment Committee*, House of Commons, © Crown Copyright 2001, Introduction, point 3.

7 *Labour Market Trends, 109*(7), July 2001, table B2 (Employment rates by age).

8 *Pensioners' incomes series 1999/2000*, DWP Analytical Services Division, 2001, Section 2, (Differences between pensioner units).

9 Ibid., section 9, table 7 (Proportion of pensioner units with less than 50% of income from state benefits, 1994/5-1999/2000).

10 *Social Security statistics 2000*, DSS, 2000, table 1 (Income support claimants by statistical group: August 1995 to August 2000).

11 *Income related benefits – estimates of take up in 1999/2000*, DWP, 2001, tables 1.1, 2.1 and 3.1.

12 *Living in Britain: results from the 2000 General Household Survey* (GHS), ONS, © Crown Copyright 2001, table 3.4 (Percentage living alone, by age and sex).

13 GHS, op. cit., Chapter 3 (Households, families and people: one person households).

14 GHS, op. cit., table 5.2(b) (Marital status by sex and age).

• This information has been developed as a result of the many enquirers who contact Age Concern England each year needing statistics on a wide range of topics of relevance to older people. It is updated annually. It gives information about older people throughout the United Kingdom but, because administrative structures are different, in some cases statistics are given for Great Britain (i.e. England, Scotland and Wales only), or in some cases England or England and Wales only. These figures are marked accordingly.

• The above information is an extract from Age Concern's web site which can be found at www.ace.org.uk

Healthy life expectancy

Estimates for 2000. Healthy Life Expectancy (HALE) summarises the expected number of years to be lived in what might be termed the equivalent of 'full health'. To calculate HALE, the years of ill-health are weighted according to severity and subtracted from the expected overall life expectancy to give the equivalent years of healthy life.

Healthy life expectancy (years)	Males	Females
Austria	68.1	72.5
Belgium	67.7	71.0
Denmark	68.9	70.1
France	68.5	72.9
Germany	67.4	71.5
Greece	69.7	72.3
Ireland	67.8	70.9
Italy	69.5	72.8
Netherlands	68.2	71.2
Norway	68.8	72.3
Portugal	63.9	68.6
Spain	68.7	72.5
Sweden	70.1	72.7
United Kingdom	**68.3**	**71.4**

Source: World Health Organisation (WHO)

Older people in Britain

Information from Counsel and Care

Introductory statistics and thoughts

In the United Kingdom in 2000 the total population was estimated to be approximately 59.7 million. Older people (men 65 and over and women 60 and over) accounted for approximately 10.8 million (18.1%) of this total. This figure is rising and by the year 2025 the population of older people is projected to rise to approximately 14.8 million. Within this total figure those 75 and over account for 4 million and this number is projected to rise to 5.9 million by 2025.

In 2000 there were 5.44 million women and 3.8 million men over the age of 65 in the UK.

Projections for the size of the older population by the year 2030 are 4.8 million men and 5.3 million women in the 65-79 age bracket and 1.5 million men and 2.3 million women aged 80 or over.

Women on average live longer than men do. Over three-quarters of people aged over 85 are women. Due to the fact that women tend to live longer a higher percentage of women than men are widowed: 62% of women over 75 are widowed compared to 29% of men. 62% of men over 75 were married compared with only 28% of women. Due to this a large number of older people live alone – 31% of men and 58% women over 75.

6% of the UK population are from minority ethnic groups, 6% of people from ethnic minority groups consist of people over the age of 60. For example 12% of the black Caribbean community are over 60 and 5% of the Pakistani community. However, this figure is set to grow rapidly over the next couple of decades since there is currently a large proportion of 'middle-aged' people within ethnic minority communities. Future service provision should be adapted to account for this. Counsel and Care has carried out research in this area.

Many older people do not work after retirement age but some do with 7% of men over 65 and 8% of women over 60 still engaged in paid work. Many other older people regularly carry out voluntary work or work as informal carers such as caring for their disabled children or partner or minding grandchildren.

The above figures are significant since they may have implications for the future provision of benefits, health care and housing.

Older age can bring both burdens and pleasures; the enjoyment of retirement and leisure time on the one hand, and on the other, ill health, low income and isolation.

Many older people still have a relatively poor standard of living and are often not recognised as making a valid contribution to society.

It is important not to consider older people as a homogeneous group; they are all individuals with widely varying needs and interests. After all we are talking about an age range from 60 to over 100! We would not make plans for 16-year-olds by looking at middle-aged people.

Perspectives on ageism. Getting the balance right

While the existence of other forms of discrimination in terms of race, gender, and disability are now widely recognised and indeed gaining in recognition, both legal and social, ageism is not established as a widespread form of discrimination and not taken as seriously. Successive governments have as yet refused to legislate against ageism, particularly in the area of employment. A private member's bill in February 1998 called for the banning of age discrimination in job advertisements.

Stereotypes about older people still prevail. This is in some ways surprising since none of us are immune to ageing, whether through caring for older relatives or friends, or through growing older ourselves.

The failure to recognise ageism is partly due to people's own fears and stereotypes. 'Old age' is often foreseen as a time of failing health (both physical and mental), poverty, and the burden of looking after parents or grandparents.

While this may be true in some cases, and we must recognise and provide for individual needs, we must also be wary of treating older people as a homogeneous and redundant grouping. There is a danger older people will begin to conform to the stereotypes created of them!

Ageism is holding preconceived ideas and stereotypes about a person because they are 'old' (usually defined as over pensionable age) and/or excluding them from services, jobs, and benefits. It may also lead to public, private or voluntary organisations failing to plan for older people because they are not considered to be a priority group.

Ageism can manifest itself in different ways. One of these ways is in the language we employ and descriptions we use of older people, including images of the way they should look and act. Ageism can also be found in the exclusion of older people, unconsciously or overtly, from certain areas of life, for example, jobs (with upper age limits), health care services, housing and benefits. This kind of discrimination is sometimes labelled institutional ageism.

In more subtle ways there are situations where the assistance given to an older person is well intended. However, stereotypes about the person being too old for certain activities or behaviour, or in need of looking after, may come into play. This attitude could for example be very patronising and frustrating for an active 85-year-old!

• The above information is an extract from *Older People in Britain: Fact and Fiction*, a factsheet from Counsel and Care. See page 41 for their address details.

The ageing of the world's population

Over the past few years, the world's population has continued on its remarkable transition path from a state of high birth and death rates to one characterised by low birth and death rates. At the heart of that transition has been the growth in the number and proportion of older persons. Such a rapid, large and ubiquitous growth has never been seen in the history of civilisation.

The current demographic revolution is predicted to continue well into the coming centuries. Its major features include the following:

- One out of every ten persons is now 60 years or above; by 2050, one out of five will be 60 years or older; and by 2150, one out of three persons will be 60 years or older.
- The older population itself is ageing. The oldest old (80 years or older) is the fastest-growing segment of the older population. They currently make up 11 per cent of the 60+ age group and will grow to 19 per cent by 2050. The number of centenarians (aged 100 years or older) is projected to increase 15-fold from approximately 145,000 in 1999 to 2.2 million by 2050.
- The majority of older persons (55 per cent) are women. Among the oldest old, 65 per cent are women.
- Striking differences exist between regions. One out of five Europeans, but one out of twenty Africans, is 60 years or older.
- In some developed countries today, the proportion of older persons is close to one in five. During the first half of the 21st century that proportion will reach one in four and in some countries one in two.
- As the tempo of ageing in developing countries is more rapid than in developed countries, developing countries will have less time than the developed countries to adapt to the consequences of population ageing.

- The majority of the world's older persons (51 per cent) live in urban areas. By 2025 this is expected to climb to 62 per cent of older persons, although large differences exist between more and less developed regions. In developed regions, 74 per cent of older persons are urban dwellers, while in less developed regions, which remain predominantly rural, 37 per cent of older persons reside in urban areas.
- Over the last half of the 20th century, 20 years were added to the average lifespan, bringing global life expectancy to its current level of 66 years. Large differences exist between countries, however. In the least developed regions, men reaching age 60 can expect only 14 more years of life and women, 16 more, while in the more developed regions, life expectancy at age 60 is 18 years for men and 22 years for women.

- The impact of population ageing is increasingly evident in the old-age dependency ratio, the number of working-age persons (age 15-64 years) per older person (65 years or older) that is used as an indicator of the 'dependency burden' on potential workers. Between 2000 and 2050, the old-age dependency ratio will double in more developed regions and triple in less developed regions. The potential socio-economic impact on society that may result from an increasing old-age dependency ratio is an area of growing research and public debate.

Source: Population Division, Department of Economic and Social Affairs, United Nations Secretariat
• The above information is from the web site of the Division for Social Policy and Development at the United Nations. See their web site at www.un.org/esa/

© *United Nations Populations Division, (United Nations, New York 2002)*

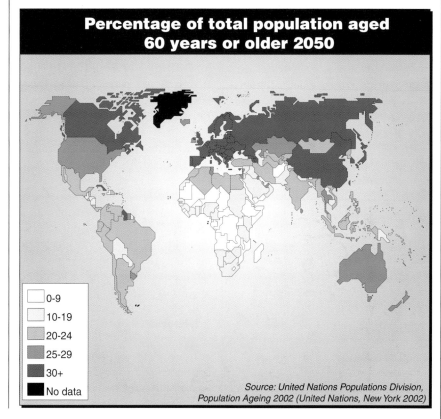

Percentage of total population aged 60 years or older 2050

- 0-9
- 10-19
- 20-24
- 25-29
- 30+
- No data

Source: United Nations Populations Division, Population Ageing 2002 (United Nations, New York 2002)

Myths and misconceptions

An ageing world

All of us have opinions about older people, and expectations – possibly fears – of our own ageing process. These may be formed from our own experiences and our relationships with older people, but are probably also affected by the many stereotypes which surround this issue. Here are some examples of the kind of myths and misconceptions which exist about ageing and older people, and some facts which challenge some of our most commonly held beliefs and views.

MYTH – *Older people are unproductive and a burden on communities and societies – especially on a working younger population*

FACT – Most people – particularly in countries where there is not a comprehensive pension system – continue to work well into old age, supporting themselves and others.

As well as the millions of older people who work for a wage, there are millions more who are unpaid workers – family and community leaders, carers of children and people who are ill, advisers, teachers, guardians of culture, volunteers . . . In both paid and unpaid work their contribution is to the development process is vital.

Some older people do need support. Older people can join together with policy makers and others in their communities to work out the best way to meet the challenges of ageing.

MYTH – *Old age starts at 60*

FACT – Sixty is generally the age at which governments and agencies start defining 'old age' but life expectancies are different in different places and there are many things which affect a person's ageing process. Some people may be 'old' at the age of 35, others are living full and productive lives after the age of 100. In many places people do not define their age in terms of how many years they have lived, but in terms of what they can do.

MYTH – *Older people are likely to be weak, frail, ill or disabled*

FACT – Some physical conditions are more likely to occur in older people, but illness and disability are NOT inevitable in old age. Generally speaking, the healthier people are throughout their life span, the less likely they will be to suffer from chronic illnesses or disabling conditions as they grow older.

MYTH – *Older people are forgetful*

FACT – The memory does change with age and older people may not remember things so fast, but the stereotype of older people being forgetful is inaccurate. There are many ways to adapt to changes in memory and many things can affect memory at any age, including stress, worry, depression or illness.

MYTH – *Older people are helpless and unable to make decisions about their own lives*

FACT – When older people do need support they generally know better than anybody else what they need. It is only in exceptional circumstances that they will be unable to make a decision or offer an opinion on what is important to them (this is true of younger people too). As well as being able to make decisions about their own lives, older people's experience is also useful when planning activities for the whole community.

MYTH – *Older people do not fall in love or have sexual relationships*

FACT – Everybody's feelings and emotions change throughout their lives, but feelings don't just stop because you grow older.

MYTH – *Older people don't enjoy their lives or have a good time*

FACT – Are you planning to stop having a good time when you grow older?

MYTH – *Older people aren't able to learn new skills or absorb new information and they do not need education or training*

FACT – Evidence suggests that older people are just as good at studying as anybody else, although they may be out of practice and may not always have the confidence in their own abilities.

It is common for older people everywhere to want to learn new skills – either to help them improve their quality of life, or help them use their free time productively. The more skills and knowledge older people have, the more they will be able to contribute to their communities.

MYTH – *Older people are somehow different to the rest of the population*

FACT – Older people are people who have lived for a long time. If we are lucky, we will all have the opportunity to grow old.

MYTH – *Expensive medical treatment is wasted on older people*

FACT – Everybody is entitled to the best medical treatment their community can provide. If older people receive medical treatment, their quality of life is maintained and they are more able to continue contributing to their communities. They are also less likely to develop serious illnesses which may require more complicated and expensive treatments.

• The above information is an extract from HelpAge International's web site which can be found at www.helpage.org. Alternatively, see page 41 for their address details.

© HelpAge International

How men in the south live longer

Men living in some parts of the United Kingdom are likely to live ten years longer than in others.

And the life expectancy gap is widening, according to figures out yesterday.

The best areas for a long life are southern England and the West Country. Environmental and living standards are high, and these regions attract many middle-class people retiring from other parts of the country.

The worst prospects are in Scotland – especially Glasgow – and in Manchester and Liverpool in the north-west.

The findings will come as a disappointment to ministers, who are pledged to cut the gap between life expectancy in the poorest areas and the national average by 10 per cent by 2010.

Looking at figures collected on a regional basis, the south-west has the healthiest record, with a life expectancy of 76.7 years for men and 81.5 for women.

Scotland emerges as the least healthy place to live, with lifespans of 72.9 years for men and 78.2 for women.

The widening gap can be seen in more detail when the records of individual health authorities are compared – the measure the Government is using for its 'health inequality target'.

Life expectancy		
By region, 1998-2000		
	Men	**Women**
South West	76.7	81.5
South East	76.6	81.1
Eastern	76.6	81.0
London	75.5	80.6
Trent	75.1	80.0
West Midlands	74.9	79.9
Wales	74.8	79.7
Northern and Yorks	74.6	79.5
Northern Ireland	74.5	79.6
North West	74.0	79.0
Scotland	72.9	78.2

Looking at these records for 1997-99, the gap for men was 7.3 years, and for women 5.3 years.

New figures for the period 1998-2000 show the gap for men had grown to 7.7 years, and for women 6.6 years.

Breaking down the statistics into local council areas, men are now living 10.3 years longer in the best than in the worst districts, and women 7.8 years.

Men's chances are best in East Dorset and women's in Westminster. For both sexes, Glasgow City offers the worst outlook.

The Office for National Statistics explained yesterday that health authorities provide a different picture because they cover bigger areas than local councils.

A spokesman said: 'Life expectancy continues to improve in the UK, but wide disparities remain between different areas.'

On average in England, a man can expect to live for 75.2 years and a woman 80.1 years.

© The Daily Mail March, 2001

An ageing world

Information from HelpAge International

Populations are ageing in almost every country in the world

In 1950, there were 200 million older people. Now there are 550 million. By 2025, there will be 1.2 billion. The speed of change is without precedent.

Nearly 80% of this increase took place in the developing world.

All of us have opinions about older people, and expectations – possibly fears – of our own ageing process. These may be formed from our own experiences and our relationships with older people, but are probably also affected by the many stereotypes which surround this issue.

We can plan for changes in population balance

Unlike other major social and economic changes, we can predict future numbers of older people with a considerable degree of confidence.

Today, most older people (61%) live in developing countries. By 2025, the number of older people will double to 850 million, proportionally 70% of older people worldwide.

Poverty remains the greatest challenge to older people. If old age is not to be synonymous with endemic poverty then policies and resources need to be redirected to support older people now.

Poverty

Worldwide, poverty in old age is linked to poor diet, ill health, inadequate housing and isolation.

In developing countries, where older populations are growing fastest, older people are consistently and disproportionately among the poorest of the poor.

Ageing is a women's issue . . .

Worldwide, women live longer than men. They make up two-thirds of the global population over 80 – and as life expectancy rises, this proportion will increase.

Compared with men, women have more chance of being widowed, and of having had poor education, nutrition and access to services in earlier life.

. . . but also poses challenges for men

Loss of earning power can have serious consequences for men's household and community status, self-respect and well-being.

Male life expectancy in the Russian Federation fell as the economy tumbled in the early 1990s, due to fewer jobs, reduced welfare provision, greater poverty, and increased alcoholism.

Conflicts and disasters put older people at special risk

Older people are a vulnerable but neglected refugee group – seldom targeted by humanitarian agencies' relief efforts and services.

Rehabilitation and reconstruction programmes should support older people's wishes to be independent and to support wider family and social efforts.

Traditional relationships between generations are changing fast

Worldwide, fewer children are shouldering the care of increasingly long-lived, dependent parents.

Chronic poverty and the scattering of families in search of work are eroding traditional patterns of care for older relatives

Older people have become key carers in families hit by HIV/AIDS

Older people now care for half of all AIDS orphans. In sub-Saharan Africa, older people are now looking after 7.8 million orphaned children.

Older people are also vulnerable to infection; they are often ignorant about the disease and suffer untreated.

Work remains critical to many older people's survival

Half the world's older people support themselves through informal labour such as childcare, trading or small-scale agriculture – all invisible in official statistics.

State pension schemes can benefit whole communities, but are rare. Occupational schemes do not reach the many poor older people whose work has been in the informal sector.

● The above information is an extract from HelpAge International's web site which can be found at www.helpage.org. Alternatively, see page 41 for their address details.

© HelpAge International

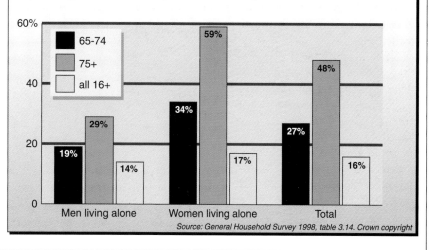

Elderly people living alone

39% of the elderly population live alone in the UK. Women, especially those over 75, are more likely than men to live alone.

Legend: 65-74, 75+, all 16+

Men living alone: 19% (65-74), 29% (75+), 14% (all 16+)
Women living alone: 34% (65-74), 59% (75+), 17% (all 16+)
Total: 27% (65-74), 48% (75+), 16% (all 16+)

Source: General Household Survey 1998, table 3.14. Crown copyright

Fit and fifty?

The executive summary of a report by the Economic and Social Research Council

- Those in their 50s will increase over the next ten years. More of them will live alone, but there will be a decline in the percentage of single men and women who are widowed in this age category.
- The percentage of those in their 50s who are divorced or separated has more than doubled over the past 20 years.
- The proportion of 50-59-year-old men who are full-time employees has fallen from around 93 per cent in the 1970s to 75 per cent in 1996. For women the figure has remained constant at around 60 per cent.
- Men in their 50s are likely to experience longer periods of unemployment and economic inactivity. Ill health is also inclined to be pronounced. There are occupational differences in these patterns.
- There is evidence of wide polarisation in wealth within the 50-59 age group. Differences in wealth levels are driven by occupational position and marital status.
- Lifestyles and leisure patterns of those in their 50s are surprisingly similar to those in their 30s and 40s. It is only in the 60s age category that age, *per se*, appears to impact upon lifestyle activities. Age in itself is no longer the predictor.
- Outright home ownership is higher among those in their 50s than among younger age groups.
- One-third of men and one-quarter of women in the 50s age group use home-based computers.

Lifestyles and leisure patterns of those in their 50s are surprisingly similar to those in their 30s and 40s. It is only in the 60s age category that age, per se, appears to impact upon lifestyle activities

---

- Health condition deteriorates with age, with this tendency being greater amongst men than women. But visits to GPs are not significantly greater among those in their 50s compared with other age groups. But, again, occupational categories are significant in these patterns, as is whether or not a person is living alone.
- With some relatively minor exceptions, the attitudes of men and women in their 50s are similar to those in their 30s and 40s. This is in terms of attitudes towards the family, gender roles, the economy and the welfare state. But those in their 50s are more concerned than younger age groups about unemployment and the quality of the environment.
- Tracking individuals over time indicates that moving out of employment reduces stress levels of professional men and women in their 50s but increases it for those in manual unskilled occupations. Health condition also improves amongst professional and managerial employees who leave employment, but deteriorates for unskilled and manual workers who lose their jobs. Unemployment in their 50s correlates with a reduction in smoking for all occupational groups.

Over-50s statistics

Information from the Association of Retired and Persons Over 50

- In common with the rest of the European Union (EU), the United Kingdom has an ageing population. In 1901 about one person in 20 was aged 65 or over and just over one person in 100 was aged 75 or over. This increased to just over one in six and about one in 14 respectively by 1998. Projections suggest that by 2016, it is expected that, for the first time, the number of people aged 65 and over will exceed those aged under 16.

- Falls in death rates have contributed to a considerable increase in the number of people living to the age of 100 or over during the second half of the 20th century. In 1951 there were fewer than 300 centenarians alive in England and Wales; this has risen to about 5,500 in 2000. This increase has been largest among women. While the numbers of centenarians are still fairly small, the rate of increase has been very large at about seven per cent each year, roughly doubling every decade. Projections suggest that the number of centenarians will continue to rise this century. By 2036 there could be over 40,000 centenarians alive in England and Wales.

- More than 25 per cent of people in the UK, US, Japan and the EU will be over 60 years old by 2015

- The over-50s, growing in number by 50,000 every month – due to the 'baby boomer' generation – have an annual income in excess of £160bn and they spend £145bn of it!

- A 50-year-old typically has half of his or her adult life still ahead of them.

- Men aged 65 and over made up 13 per cent of the total male population in 1998.

- Women aged 65 and over made up 18 per cent of the total female population in 1998.

- The ratio of females to males increases with age. Women currently begin to outnumber men from around the age of 50 and by the age of 89 there are about three women to every man.

- It is not uncommon nowadays for the post-work phase of life to span 24 years, which is a sixfold increase on the recent past when you worked to 65 and died perhaps four years later.

- In 1998/1999, about 50 per cent of one-person households in Great Britain were comprised of people over pensionable age.

- Those currently aged from 45 to 54 have the highest level of pension scheme membership with 84 per cent of men and 70 per cent of women in full-time jobs being in either occupational or pension schemes.

- Sixty-two per cent of men and women over age of 65 have a current account. Fifty-seven per cent have a building society account. Fifteen per cent have stocks and shares. Sixteen per cent have premium bonds. Eight per cent have TESSAs. Seven per cent have PEPs.

- Barclays estimate that of the 50,000 new business start-ups annually by the over-50s (which represent ten per cent of the national total) the success rate is much higher than average, with seven out of 10 still in business after five years.

- Those aged between 50 and 64 represent the biggest spenders in absolute terms on fuel and power, alcoholic drinks, motoring, leisure goods and leisure services.

- The strongest loyalty to brands such as Waitrose and Marks & Spencer is among the 45+ age group.

- Older people watch more television than younger people – people aged 65 and over watched about twice as much television as children aged 4 to 15 on average. Around 13 to 14 per cent of people aged 65 and over watched news programmes compared with only about 9 per cent of those aged 16 to 44. Overall, drama programmes are the most commonly watched types of television programme.

- Older people are more likely than younger people to read the *Daily Mail*, *Daily Express* and *Daily Telegraph*.

- In 1998, about one in five people in Great Britain reported that they had done unpaid charitable work in the previous year.

- The proportion of households in Great Britain with a home computer almost doubled between 1988 and 1998-99, from 18 per cent to 34 per cent. Surveys by Microsoft show that the over-50s spend more time on-line than other age groups.

- In 1998, 56 million holidays of four nights or more were taken by British residents, a third more than in 1971.

- Those aged 45 to 54 years were the most likely people to take a holiday abroad.

- In America, the 55-plus age group now accounts for over 40 per cent of all health club memberships.

- According to the *General Household Survey*, 68 per cent of men and 59 per cent of women aged 45-59 participate in at least one physical activity and very similar figures continue right up to age 70.

- Like the UK, the over-50s dominate many consumer markets in mainland Europe, accounting for 45 per cent of all new cars (80 per cent of 'top of the range' cars), 55 per cent of the coffee market, 50 per cent of the mineral water, 50 per cent of skincare preparations and 35 per cent of all tourism.
- The over-50s group represents 40 per cent of consumer spending – £145 billion a year.
- Sixty per cent of all UK savings and investments are held by people over the age of 50.

The over-50s group represents 40 per cent of consumer spending – £145 billion a year

---

- The average household income after tax for the over-50s group is £36,000 (against £20,000 for the rest of the population).
- Eighty per cent of all e-commerce transactions are carried out by people over the age of 45. Three and a half million of those over 50 regularly use the internet in Britain. (This group is the fastest-growing internet user group.)
- Over-50s make up a third of all voters and of those certain to vote in the next General Election, 46 per cent are aged over 50.

• The above information is an extract from the Association of Retired and Persons Over 50s web site which can be found at www.arp050.org.uk Alternatively, see page 41 for their address details.

How the over-60s are taking over the world

By Bill Bond

The world needs to make better use of its older people to solve the problems of an ageing population, an international conference was told yesterday.

By the year 2050 the number of over-60s will have increased from the present 600 million to two billion – one in five of the global total.

For the first time, senior citizens will outnumber the under-15s almost everywhere, not just in developed countries, said Spanish social affairs minister Juan Carlos Aparicio, speaking on behalf of the EU.

He told delegates from 160 nations and international bodies the change will make unprecedented demands on society, ranging from ensuring adequate pensions, housing and health care to protecting the elderly from discrimination and abuse.

Experts say the process will be most dramatic in developing nations, where social security systems are less well equipped to shield the old from neglect and abuse.

The UN World Assembly on Ageing, being held in Madrid, aims to agree strategies to help the elderly and include them more actively within society.

Spanish prime minister Jose Maria Aznar, the current president of the EU, said governments needed to keep their ageing populations active with continued education and what he called 'flexible work schedules'.

He added: 'Making good use of the potential of older people will be vital to help meet the rising costs deriving from the new population structure.'

UN Secretary-General Kofi Annan took pains to stress that a rapidly greying world presented opportunities as well as challenges.

'As more people are better educated, live longer and stay healthy longer, older persons can and do make greater contributions to society than ever before,' he said.

The conference heard that, by 2050, worldwide expectancy will have gone up from the present 66 years to 77.

'As more people are better educated, live longer and stay healthy longer, older persons can and do make greater contributions to society than ever before'

There are fears that the pace of change could have devastating effects on poor countries.

The latest UN statistics show the percentage of older people is growing faster in developing countries, already burdened with the fight against poverty and Aids.

In France, for example, the elderly population took 140 years to grow from 9 per cent to 14 per cent. In less-developed countries, the figure is expected to explode from 8 per cent now to 20 per cent in under 50 years.

Yet even the prosperous US and Europe, where over-60s already outnumber under-15s, are having problems over retirement and health care systems. 'If this is a problem in developed countries, imagine what it means for poor countries,' said UN official Nitin Desai.

The explosion in the number of older people is coming just as more people migrate from rural areas into cities looking for work, eroding traditional family support networks.

'Older persons in rural areas in many African countries are struggling to cope and fend for themselves in order to survive,' said Ghana's employment minister Cecilia Bannerman.

Ageing issues

All older people have the right to expect later life to be a fulfilling and enjoyable experience whatever their personal circumstances. We know that the number of people over pensionable age is set to rise: by 2021 there will be 12 million people aged over 65 years.

We will also see a corresponding decrease in the number of younger people in society. The make-up of the population is changing and with it we will see the political and economic power of older people increase as the 'baby boomers' demand better health, social care and leisure services.

Issues affecting today's older people and those in the future, need to be addressed by policy makers: the voices of older people are growing.

Some key issues

Age discrimination
Older people face discrimination in employment, in health care, and as consumers. Successive governments have legislated against discrimination by gender, religion, race and disability, but have not done so for age. The present government produced a voluntary Code of Practice against age discrimination in employment but this does nothing to penalise its perpetrators or compensate victims.

However, the government recently launched the National Service Framework for Older People, and Standard 1 of the Framework states, 'NHS services will be provided, regardless of age, on the basis of clinical need alone. Social Care services will not use age in their eligibility criteria or policies, to restrict access to available services.'

Age Concern believes in the concept of 'age neutrality'.

Income
According to government figures, more than half of the nation's single pensioners have net incomes of less than £90 a week. A quarter of couples

have net incomes of less than £135 a week. Age Concern England commissioned research to establish the incomes which older people need to avoid poverty and achieve an 'acceptable' standard of living. The figures ranged from £99 to £125 a week for single people and from £149 to £184 for couples. Pensioner poverty is aggravated by the low take-up of many means-tested benefits.

Health
The health needs of older people cannot be divorced from their level of income and housing conditions. If older people are poor, ill-housed and socially excluded, they are more likely to become physically and mentally ill. In addition, recent research undertaken by Age Concern England identified the existence of age discrimination within NHS. This is unacceptable.

Social exclusion
Older people are a valuable resource to our society and yet are very often socially excluded from everyday activities and services. As individual citizens they have the right to equality of opportunity to an adequate income and services to enable them to lead a fulfilling and enjoyable life.

Active citizens
Older people have a wealth of knowledge and experience that can be utilised to the benefit of society as a whole. This valuable resource should be 'tapped' by government and recognised and respected by society.

Employment and lifelong learning
Opportunities should be made available to people aged 50 and over to continue in paid employment if this is what they wish to do; and have access to educational and training opportunities to learn new skills and gain new knowledge.

• The above information is an extract from Age Concern's web site which can be found at www.ace.org.uk

© 2002 Age Concern England

Seniors in the media

Older people are underrepresented or misrepresented in the media with seniors either categorised as Victor Meldrews or Joan Collinses – neither of which is a true reflection of the vast majority within our age group.

Now that BBC research has come to the same conclusion it is committed to making changes for the better. The Association's Director of Social Policy, Don Steele, welcomes this opportunity to confront the problem head-on and plan for the future.

'Seniors represent a growing audience but what older people want to see, and how they are portrayed, has still largely been sidelined,' he claimed.

The BBC admits that over-55s remain chronically underrepresented on television by some 50 per cent and older women fare even worse with men outnumbering women by a ratio of three to one.

'Seniors are primarily interested in health, travel and leisure, keeping fit and acquiring new skills through part- or full-time study, with considerable numbers taking an active interest in financial matters, yet there are few programmes tackling these subjects in a way that is specifically targeted to our age group,' he pointed out.

'Many members also object to the way that older people are portrayed as victims of crime or allowed to participate in drama only as minor characters or passive observers,' he continued, 'but now that our own anecdotal evidence has been supported by concrete research findings from the BBC itself, we can work towards a fairer representation of what we would like to see on television to the benefit of all concerned.'

The USA – where hundreds of seniors now write, produce and 'star' in their own public access programmes ranging from AGEility (the art of re-inventing ourself

presented by a 73-year-old Florida woman) to other small stations where whole teams of writers, researchers, producers and presenters consist entirely of older people – could provide a valuable pointer to the way ahead for post-Millennium Britain, Mr Steele suggested.

The Internet, too, is playing a growing part in disseminating news from older people to older people: American ARP's Seniornet website,

---

'Seniors represent a growing audience but what older people want to see, and how they are portrayed, has still largely been sidelined'

---

for instance, attracts more than one million hits a week.

As a new digital dawn approaches, the BBC has thrown down the gauntlet by challenging older people to respond with what we want to see, how we want to be portrayed and how we feel we can become involved in programme origination and execution in the years to come. Our response will govern not only how seniors view each other, but also how society views us.

If you have a point of view or a special skill which could be of help to the Association in putting across a positive image of older people, please send full details to Don Steele, Director, ARP/050, Greencoat House, Francis Street, London SW1P 1DZ. Or e-mail us on info@arp.org.uk

• The above information is an extract from the Association of Retired and Persons Over 50's web site which can be found at www.arp050.org.uk Alternatively, see page 41 for their address details.

How pensioners are treated in the UK and in Europe

1. In Belgium, pensioners receive 60 per cent of average earnings compared to 15 per cent in the UK.
2. In France, it's 70 per cent.
3. In Greece, 80 per cent of last two years' average earnings.
4. In Holland, £150 per week.
5. Italian pensioners receive 83 per cent of their last five years' average earnings.
6. Over-60s in Ireland get free travel on buses and trains.
7. There are no standing charges for Irish pensioners on utilities.
8. Spanish pensioners get free tickets to theatres and cinemas.
9. Spanish and Irish pensioners watch TV for free.
10. There are state-run pension clubs in Spain.

• The above information is from the Graphical Paper Media Union's (GPMU) web site which can be found at www.gpmu.org.uk

CHAPTER TWO: AGEISM IN THE WORKPLACE

Age discrimination

Information from the Work Foundation

Definition

Age discrimination occurs when employers make decisions affecting procedures for advertising, recruitment, selection, promotion, training and development on the basis of individuals' age rather than their skills, abilities, qualifications and potential.

- Much research is concerned with discrimination against the over-50s, but job adverts frequently give age limits of 40, 35 or even 30.

Background

- As the sex and race discrimination legislation of the 1970s and 1980s has become more widely accepted, people have become more aware of those groups which are not legally covered, i.e. older workers and people with disabilities.

Reasons for age discrimination are:

- Recession – organisations' reductions in the size of the workforce concentrated on early retirement first and targeted redundancy at older workers.
- Younger employees are generally cheaper to employ.
- Young employees are thought to be more flexible and more skilled in technology.
- Older workers are thought to be more costly for benefits, such as sick leave and pensions, as well as salary.

However, organisations are now beginning to see the results of age discrimination:

- When older employees leave, their knowledge, skills and experience go too.
- Mixed age groups provide balance.
- Older customers, clients and suppliers may prefer dealing with older employees in retail, insurance, banking and other service industries.

Key facts

By the year 2050 almost a quarter of the population will be aged over 65. Yet economic activity rates for those over 50 are declining. According to government statistics:

- For men aged 50 to 64 the activity rate was 68.4% in 1995 (in 1975 the rate for men aged 55 to 59 was 94%).
- For women aged 50 to 59 in 1995 the rate was 63.9% but these rates are not declining – due perhaps to the increase in job opportunities, particularly part time, for women.
- Rates for those over retirement age drop dramatically: men 9%, married women 5% and non-married women 3%.
- Of those who do work, older people are most likely to work part time. In 1994:
  – of those aged 50 to 59 more than a quarter of those who worked were part time.
  – of those aged 60 to 64, 35.5% were part time.

– for the over-65s, 70.4% were part time.
– older people are more likely to be self-employed: of those aged 50 to state pension age, 17% were self-employed (all employees: 12.8%).

- A study of 4000 job adverts by Industrial Relations Services in 1993 found that almost one-third required applications to be 45 or under. Some specified 35 or under.
- A study of the views of candidates and employers by Sanders & Sidney revealed that career prospects started to be limited at age 42.
- The cost of replacement: W. H. Smith calculated that it costs £2,500 to replace a sales assistant.
- B&Q, which decided to staff an entire store with over-50s as an experiment to demonstrate the capabilities of older employees, found that staff turnover was six times lower than average, absenteeism was 39% lower and profitability turnover was up 18%. B&Q continues to recruit older workers but into mixed-age stores.

State of play

- There is no direct legislation on age discrimination in the UK. However, age-based selection for redundancy has been found to be unlawful (Walker, Nolan and Kiddy v Carbodies Ltd) and an age limit affecting more of one sex than the other could be seen as indirect discrimination under the Sex Discrimination Act 1975.
- About 100 large UK companies joined the Third Age Programme (organised by the Carnegie Foundation). Of these 20 have formally changed policies to end age discrimination.
- The Employers' Forum on Age

(EFA) was set up in 1996. It is a network for employers to promote mixed-age workforces. The Industrial Society is a founder member. It provides information, auditing methods, research and so on.

- The POPE project (People of Previous Experience) was set up by the Bradford & District TEC to help the unemployed over-50s get jobs. It created a register of such people and a list of employers with suitable vacancies. It matched candidates with available jobs and paid employers £2,000 for each job filled. In a year it made 110 placements.
- The age limit has now been dropped to 40, people have been given support and training and employers no longer receive the subsidy.

Best practice guidelines

Age discrimination reduces an organisation's effectiveness, and, with a growing older population, gives a bad image.

- Recruitment policy should be to recruit the best staff, regardless of age. Organisations' employees should reflect the diversity of their existing and potential customers.
- To retain knowledge and experience the organisation needs to attract and retain a proportion of older employees.
- Reorganisations and redundancies should be planned so that appropriate, and not just older, employees are targeted.
- Recruitment, training, development and promotion should be on the basis of experience and aptitude, not age.
- Challenge stereotypes – many older workers like computers, welcome a challenge, and want to try something new.
- Capitalise on investments in training and development for employees in all age groups.
- Avoid 'ghettos' of older workers – create mixed-age teams.

• The above information is an extract from a Management Factsheet, produced by the Work Foundation (formerly the Industrial Society).

© The Work Foundation

Age – the issues for today's workplace

Information from the Employers' Forum on Age

Government and employers now have less than six years in which to shape and prepare for age discrimination legislation.

But while legislation has a role to play in challenging age prejudice and stereotypes, on its own it is not enough to tackle age discrimination. It will be making a clear business case for age diversity which will have the greatest impact on employers. The EFA's new *Business Case for Age Diversity*, launched on 24 January 2002, does just this.

People are living longer than ever before and are having fewer children. As a result, our population is ageing, and this is happening around the rest of the developed world. From an employment perspective, the dramatic drop in numbers of young people coming into the labour market is beginning to have a huge impact on the pool from which employers are able to recruit new employees.

Ageism is widespread and affects all age groups. Some define an older worker as a 'woman over 35' and 'a man over 42'. Very recently a leading IT analyst told suppliers to sack all their staff aged over 50 as they are too old to be retrained. At the other end of the scale, a 27-year-old secretary with 9 years' experience may be considered too young for a post, despite having sufficient experience.

Employment decisions such as these do not make good business sense.

Age discrimination affects all aspects of employment, not just recruitment. EFA research clearly shows that promotion, training as well as redundancy and retirement selection can all be affected when decisions are based on age.

The business benefits of a mixed-age workforce are now widely recognised. There is clear evidence that both turnover and absenteeism are reduced and that motivation and commitment are improved in organisations employing people of all ages.

Ageism is wide-spread and affects all age groups

EFA aims to promote good practice among employers. We do not promote positive discrimination in favour of older workers. Nor do we advocate employing older workers instead of younger workers.

Employment law has for some time allowed for age discrimination to be challenged, but the introduction of a Code of Practice in the UK in 1999, and now the prospect of legislation by 2006 guarantees that this issue will remain high on the employment agenda.

Ageism is deeply entrenched in society and the workplace. Valuing people of all ages within the workforce and regarding them all as a sustainable rather than a disposable resource is essential for our future prosperity. Collaboration between the Government and employers is key to making a difference. EFA will continue to press for meaningful change and top-level commitment to eradicate age discrimination from employment.

• The above information is an extract from the Employers' Forum on Age's web site: www.efa.org.uk

© 2002 The Employers' Forum on Age

Now you're over the hill at 42

By Ben Summerskill, Society Editor

Life does not begin at forty. Age discrimination at work is becoming an even younger habit with people in their early forties now ranked alongside much older people in being considered over the hill by employers.

For decades, workers in their fifties have complained about being thought of as surplus to requirements in the job market. But one in four adults now thinks that employers are no longer interested in taking on the over-forties.

'We're now establishing that age discrimination starts as early as 42,' said Patrick Grattan of the Third Age Employment Network. 'Evidence is growing of a dramatic drop in the number of people employed once they become older. It's not only a question of people not getting jobs. Even when they do, they're being paid at a discount. That discount is purely a matter of prejudice.'

Fifty per cent of companies now have workforces with fewer than one in ten staff over 50. Ten per cent of firms had no employees over 50.

'I have decades of experience in both business and human resources. I managed to bring up children at the same time,' said Anna Evans-Pollard from Chepstow. 'But people don't take you seriously at all at a certain age. They don't actually say they want someone younger. You just know it.'

Theo Blackwell, a specialist in workplace discrimination at the Industrial Society, said: 'Too many firms have a constant emphasis on restructuring. This all too often means that workers who are 40-plus are getting pushed out to make way for younger people. They are thought to be more flexible and adaptable to technology. It doesn't follow at all.'

But employers will soon have little choice but to start treating middle-aged staff more sympathetically. The number of people aged between 16 and 19 has already fallen by 13.1 per cent since 1991 as the fertility rate has plummeted to 1.7 children from its peak level of 2.8 children in the early 1960s.

Workplace economists estimate the loss to the economy caused by the exclusion of older people from the labour market is up to £26 billion a year but a proposed European equal treatment directive would outlaw age discrimination in the workplace from 2006, following similar schemes in Ireland, France and the Netherlands.

- This article appeared in *The Observer*, Sunday 3 March, 2002.

Useful facts and figures

- Age discrimination costs the UK £31 billion a year
- By 2006 there will be more 55-64-year-olds than 16-24-year-olds for the first time
- Between 1986 and 2006, the number of men aged 16-24 is predicted to fall by 26%, and the number of women by 30%
- Between 1986 and 2006, the numbers of 35-44-year-old men will increase by 19% and the number of women in this age group by 39%
- By 2006, 45-59-year-olds will form the largest group in the labour force
- There are 1 million fewer people in their 20s than ten years ago
- 68% of employers seeking skilled staff are experiencing recruitment difficulties
- 95% of 55-65-year-old men were working in 1975. In 1999 it was close to 60%
- Life expectancy increases one more year approximately every four years
- 75% of people in Local Government employment are retiring early
- 95% of 55-65-year-old men were working in 1975. In 1999 it was close to 60%
- Nine out of 10 people aged 50 and over receive no training from their employer at all
- At least 40% of people who retired early feel that they were forced to against their will and would rather have continued to work
- A significant proportion of IT professionals think the term older worker can be applied to someone younger than 35
- Close to half of young workers say they've been held back at work because of their age

• The above information is an extract from the Employers' Forum on Age's web site which can be found at www.efa.org.uk

Key facts on age diversity and employment

In the last 25 years there has been a dramatic decline in work after age 50: fewer working people have to support more non-working people. Company restructuring, early retirement/ redundancy and age discrimination have caused this at a time of growing life expectancy.

- Life expectancy increases one more year approximately every four years; there are 1 million fewer people in their 20s than ten years ago; (Office for National Statistics)
- in the decade 1991-2001 there has been a 1.5 million increase in the numbers of 50-64-year-olds; (Office for National Statistics)
- only 50% of unqualified men over age 50 are working; (Employment Policy Institute)
- 84% of men over age 50 were working in 1979; 69% were working in 2000; (Labour Force Statistics)
- 600,000 more men over age 50 and 200,000 more women over age 50 would be working now if older men worked at the level of 1979 and if older women had shared in the increase in work for younger women; (London School of Economics)
- the economy would be 10% larger today if employment patterns for over-50s were the same as 20 years ago; (Lombard Street Research)
- the cost of age discrimination to the economy is £5.5 billion to Government tax and benefits and £31 billion in lost production; (Cranfield School of Management for EFA)
- job insecurity has increased: temporary employment increased by 40% in the decade to 1997 and half of the jobs taken up on return to work end within six months. (Labour Force Statistics)

Stereotypes about age are widespread.

- 9 out of 10 older people believe that employers discriminate on grounds of age; (NOP research – Code on Age Diversity)
- long-term unemployment increases with age: 50% of long-term unemployed over-50s do not return to work; (Labour Force Statistics)
- age discrimination starts at 42; (Sanders and Sidney survey)
- successive generations are leaving work earlier; (Cabinet Office Performance and Innovation Unit)
- 55% of managers say that they used age as a criterion for recruitment; (Institute of Management survey)
- a survey of employers showed that in 50% of companies the over-50s made up less than 10% of the workforce, although they represent 30% of people of working age; (Institute of Directors)
- three-quarters of UK Companies have no employees over 60; (Norwich Union research)
- official retirement age is irrelevant to two-thirds of the population who leave work before that date: 70% of men over age 60 are on pension or benefits.

Discrimination leads to under-achievement, low self-esteem, individuals giving up, poor health and exclusion.

- 25% of over-50s want full-time work and looked for it when first out of work: a year later only 2% were looking for work as a result of the barriers they experienced; (Sheffield Hallam University)
- training decreases with age: there is a 50% reduction in training levels for over-50s compared to 35-50-year-olds; (New Policy Institute)
- qualifications decrease with age: 40% of non-working 50+ men have no formal qualifications; 50+

Employment status by age

Less than 40 per cent of those aged 55-64 are currently in paid work, compared to 75 per cent of those aged between 45 to 54. The lowest level of paid employment is found among those aged 65 and over (6 per cent) and the highest among these aged 25-34 (85 per cent). Older respondents are more likely than other age groups to participate in unpaid voluntary work (15 per cent of those aged 65 plus).

Employment status by age

	Total Base: 1,004	16-24 years Base: 177	25-34 years Base: 195	35-44 years Base: 173	45-54 years Base: 144	55-64 years Base: 126	65+ years Base: 190
In paid work	59%	65%	85%	80%	75%	39%	6%
Unpaid voluntary work	6%	2%	3%	0%	9%	8%	15%
Not in paid work	35%	33%	12%	20%	16%	52%	79%

Source: This material is taken from *Age Discrimination at Work* by Melissa Compton-Edwards (Jun 01), with the permission of the publisher, the Chartered Institute of Personnel and Development, London

women have three times fewer qualifications than men; (Labour Force Statistics)

- job-sharing and flexible working is less common amongst older people when it should be more common; (Work Foundation)
- a 50+ redundant male is 50% more likely to die of respiratory diseases than a working male; (NHS Statistics)
- non-working people visit the doctor three times more than those in work; (NHS Statistics)
- depressive disorders are 50% higher amongst non-workers and rise with age and low qualifications; (NHS Statistics)
- non-working people are less, rather than more, likely to participate in other activities such as volunteering, caring or learning; (Cabinet Office Performance and Innovation Unit)
- people with no formal qualifications are half as likely to participate in learning and twice as many over-50s have no qualifications as those under age 50. (NIACE and Labour Force Statistics)

Age prejudice and poverty are closely related.

- Life expectancy in poor neighbourhoods is eight years less than in wealthy neighbourhoods; (Office for National Statistics)
- inequality of wealth is greater among workless over-50s than in the working population: 57% of workless people are in households without occupational pensions and 40% of them are in the lowest fifth of income distribution, with an average income of £72 per week; (DSS)
- most occupational pensions are small: 50% are in the range £3,000 to £7,000 a year, although the income from all sources of the top 20% is £30,000+; (DSS/Cabinet Office)
- in the age group 45-64, 48% of unskilled men have a limiting disability compared to 17% of professional men.

Hidden unemployment is more important than 'official' unemployment.

- There are eight people aged 50-65 who are 'economically inactive' for every one registered unemployed. There are 1 million 'hidden unemployed' 50-64-year-olds in addition to the 0.3 million registered unemployed over-50s; (Cranfield School of Management. Sheffield Hallam University)
- there are over 1.5 million over-50s on some form of incapacity benefit, but 75% say they could do some types of work; (Sheffield Hallam University)
- the numbers who are dependent on long-term sickness and disability benefit have increased 300% in seven years, at a time when national health statistics are improving; (Office for National Statistics)
- 75% of people in Local Government employment are retiring early, 40% of them on grounds of ill health, at an average age of 54. (Audit Commission)

Age diversity in the workforce makes commercial sense.

- Halifax Building Society increased profits by £130,000

at 6 Branches trialling an older workforce; (Halifax for EFA)
- Nationwide saved £7 million in staff turnover costs by widening the recruitment age; (Nationwide for EFA)
- B&Q's Macclesfield Store, staffed entirely by people over age 50, achieved 18% more profit, 39% less absenteeism and 59% less shrinkage than benchmarked stores; (B&Q)
- 80% of the population think employing older people is good for the company image and that age is no barrier to learning new skills; (NOP survey for FiftyOn)
- 'Employing people of a certain age has been a boon to our company'; (The Heavenly Bed Company, Maidstone)
- older workers do not cost more: people returning to work after a gap earn 25% less than before they left the workforce; (London School of Economics)
- absence through sickness is not higher amongst older people; (Employers Forum on Age)
- increasing numbers of companies are responding to skills shortages with older worker recruitment and retention.

Older people can succeed in a fresh start.

- Individual flexibility about the choice of work does not decrease with age; (Social Focus on Older People, Office for National Statistics)
- over-50s taking part in government training programmes are more committed and achieve better results, although starting with a lower level of formal qualifications; (Training older People, QPID, DfEE)
- small businesses started by people aged 50+ are twice as likely to succeed as businesses started by younger people; (Warwick Business School)
- people aged over 50 are signing on to the Internet at double the rate of under-30s; (Microsoft);
- small and medium-sized businesses (over 90% of all businesses) show less age discrimination than larger hierarchical businesses; (Humberside TEC)
- members of the Third Age Employment Network help many thousands of mature people into new roles every year.

The above information is from the Third Age Employment Network's web site which can be found at www.taen.org.uk Alternatively, see page 41 for their address details.

© Third Age Employment Network

Learning to value experience

By Margaret Hughes

One key message from the debate on the future of pensions is that more and more of us are going to have to work for longer if we are to provide enough income for ourselves in retirement.

Given that most people now leaving work between 50 and state retirement age are not doing so voluntarily, with twice as many 55 to 64-year-olds being made redundant or forced to take early retirement as workers in any other age group, how will that be possible?

For, with ageism still widespread, their chances of getting another job are still slim, let alone getting a job with a comparable pay package. The same goes for those who want to hang on to their jobs.

Hopes are now pinned on the new European directive which will impose age discrimination legislation from 2006. But many organisations which focus on the over-50s are concerned about the delay in implementation. Legislation to combat discrimination on grounds of gender and religion, which is also included in the EU directive, will be introduced three years earlier.

However, the good news is that a number of initiatives to address the immediate needs of over-45s who want to get back into the workplace and raise awareness among employers are beginning to have an impact.

A leading light is Experience Works!, which was launched in May last year. It operates two centres at Loughborough College and at New College Nottingham which run flexible workshops providing free training in interview techniques, confidence building, CV writing and job searching as well as in IT skills. It also acts as a broker between employers and those seeking work, which it will shortly extend online.

It plans to open other centres in the region and is liaising with organisations considering similar initiatives in other parts of the country with a view to setting up a nationwide network.

Project manager Liz Farmer says that, even though employers are experiencing increasing problems in recruiting younger employees with appropriate skills and are failing to hang on to them, they are slow to recognise the advantages of a mature workforce 'until it hits them between their eyes'.

Most people now leaving work between 50 and state retirement age are not doing so voluntarily

---

Experience Works! held a conference last week in Loughborough hosted by John Humphrys. One of the speakers was 48-year-old Dee Parker who, when she was made redundant for the fourth time after 25 years in the clothing industry (where she had risen to director level), vowed that she wouldn't go through it again.

Ms Parker enrolled on the Experience Works! course to regain her confidence. As a result, she has set up her own consultancy business and lectures in fashion technology at Nottingham Trent University. To help others gain from her experience, Ms Parker also teaches confidence building at Experience Works! centres.

Another pioneering initiative, this time by a government agency – the North Yorkshire Employment Service – was a conference with the same theme in York this week. So successful was the event in attracting employer interest, with 50% more participants than anticipated, that it looks set to be a template for similar conferences throughout the country.

This week's event was organised with the support of Target (Third Age Recruitment Guidance and Employment Training) which was set up four and a half years ago by Jim McCauley and Peter Begley after they'd lost their jobs and found ageism a barrier to finding new work. Target, which runs training courses both at its centre in York and online, has managed to find work for a very impressive 95% of the 4,500 people who have signed up for courses.

One employer in the York area which has seen the benefit of employing more mature employees is Hunters Estate Agents. Human resources director Glynnis Frew admits this happened 'more by accident than design', but says that the 'positive results' have now prompted the company to actively recruit older workers for their commitment and 'can do' attitude to work.

One of her recent recruits is 58-year-old Hugh Gillmore who says he found that, like others at managerial level, he had reached his 'sell-by date' in the food retail business where he had worked for most of his life, part of it overseas.

£31 billion per year

The cost to the UK economy of our failure to tackle ageism

- By 2025, for every two people employed there is likely to be one person older than 50 who is either retired or inactive
- Flexible retirement could boost the economically active population by 3 million, which could raise the GDP by £50 billion or more per year

A year after the Government released its *Winning the Generation Game** strategy on tackling unemployment among the over-50s, a hard-hitting report published today (27 April) by the Employers' Forum on Age warns that the cost of ageism has risen to a staggering £31 billion in lost GDP per year – a rise of £5 billion since 1998.

The report, *Ageism: Too Costly to Ignore*, reveals that in the last two years the number of people aged between 50 and 64 who are not in work and are currently not seeking work has grown by 125,000. It argues that if the UK's ageist culture is to be successfully challenged then the Government must focus on and secure tangible change in three key areas:

- Fiscal incentives must be used to replace the concept of a 'retirement age' with an extended and staged period of departure from the labour market, i.e. flexible retirement

- Employers must be encouraged to overcome stereotypes and develop a more enlightened appreciation of the contribution that older workers can make to the success of the businesses
- Older workers must be aided, with appropriate incentives, to increase their employability by investing in their skills

The findings also show that flexible retirement could boost the economically active population by 3 million or more, albeit on a part-time basis, which could raise GDP by £50 billion or more per year.

Sam Mercer, campaign director of the Employers' Forum on Age, says: 'The Government is acutely aware of the gravity of the problem and its concern has been heightened by the knowledge that the population is rapidly ageing. But while it has signed up to the EU directive to outlaw ageism in employment by 2006, it has failed to meet many of its own deadlines. One year on, it would appear that the Government is only beginning to recognise the true scale of the task it set itself in committing to the recommendations in *Winning the Generation Game*.'

Séan Rickard, of the Cranfield School of Management and author of the report, says: 'The combination of fewer young people entering the workforce, an ageing population and falling participation rates among the over-50s will actually reduce the numbers in employment by 2025. This will magnify the already significant problem of skills shortages, with an associated and negative impact on UK competitiveness, GDP and living standards for all.'

Over the next 25 years the proportion of the population aged 50 and above will rise from 33 to 41 per cent: an increase of six million. Over the same period the numbers aged between 16 and 50 will fall by 1.5 million. If the proportion of those aged 50 and above who are economically inactive remains unchanged – and it has been rising for more than 20 years – then over the next 25 years 'disguised unemployment' in this age group will rise by almost one million. This will mean that by 2025 for every two people employed there is likely to be one person older than 50 who is either retired or inactive.

* *Winning the Generation Game*, Performance and Innovation Unit, 27 April 2000

• The above information is an extract from the Employers' Forum on Age's web site which can be found at www.efa.org.uk

Experience of age discrimination

The evidence

Discrimination is by definition hard to measure. It is not overt. Often it is unconscious rather than deliberate – a reflection of attitudes and stereotypes which only change gradually.

People aged 50-64 represent:

- $\frac{1}{3}$rd of people of working age;
- $\frac{1}{5}$th of those actually in work;
- $\frac{1}{10}$th of those on employer and government training programmes.

Unemployment statistics

Government statistics highlight age discrimination. The older the person, the longer they are likely to remain unemployed. Six out of ten people under the age of 50 who have been made redundant get back into work within a year; only one out of ten people over the age of 50 who are made redundant get back into work within a year.

Training statistics

A government report showed that the over-50s arrive on training schemes with a lower level of prior formal qualifications, that they do as well as anyone else on the course but find it harder to get a job because of age barriers.

(Training Older Workers, QPID DfEE, 2000)

Age pay gaps

Those returning to the labour market following redundancy or other gap from work face a pay reduction compared to their previous job. This wage penalty has risen steadily over the last twenty years. In the case of under-50s the discount on the level of pay in a new job is 12% compared to pay in the last job. For those over age 45 it is now 26%, up from 12% in 1980 and reflecting prejudices about older workers.

(The Journal of The Centre for Economic Performance, 2001; Campbell, LSE, 1999)

Research evidence

Eden Brown employee survey, October 2001:
A survey of 1,150 employees found that discrimination at work on the basis of age was more common than on grounds of gender or race.

Industrial Relations Service (IRS), July 2001:
A survey of 105 firms employing over 1 million people found that the voluntary Code of Practice on Age Diversity in Employment had not changed the scene, that there is little or no training for over-50s and that half of employees retire early.

Kingston University (Mark Hart), May 2001:
A Third Age and Enterprise survey of clients of 140 Enterprise Agencies and Business Links found that age discrimination was a universal problem in the redundancy process.

NOP evaluation survey, Spring 2001:
Evaluating the Government's voluntary Code of Practice on Age Diversity in Employment, NOP found that:

- 9 out of 10 older people believe that employers discriminate against older employees;
- 1 in 4 people have personally experienced age discrimination.

CIPD Age Discrimination at Work, January 2001:
In a survey of over 1,000 people the Chartered Institute of Personnel and Development found that:

- 1 in 8 workers had been discouraged from applying from jobs on grounds of age;
- 1 in 4 think that employers are not interested in employing people over age 40.

Silicon Research Services, October 2000:
In a study of the IT industry, two-thirds of a sample of 1,400 IT professionals thought they would be unable to get a job past age 45. Union Network International, the authors, concluded that ageism is 'rife'. Although two-thirds of IT firms have difficulty recruiting, ageism was assessed as having an impact after age 35.

NOP Monitoring the Code, June 2000:
In its monitoring of the impact of the voluntary Code of Practice on

Redundancies

One in ten 55-64 year-olds were made redundant in the last year – a higher proportion than for any other age group

Percentage who have been made redundant in the last 12 months, by age

	Total Base: 1,004	16-24 years Base: 177	25-34 years Base: 195	35-44 years Base: 173	45-54 years Base: 144	55-64 years Base: 126	65+ years Base: 190
All who have been made redundant	5%	5%	5%	6%	5%	10%	1%
Have been made compulsorily redundant	3%	4%	3%	5%	3%	7%	1%
Have taken voluntary redundancy	1%	1%	2%	1%	2%	2%	1%

Source: This material is taken from *Age Discrimination at Work* by Melissa Compton-Edwards (Jun 01), with the permission of the publisher, the Chartered Institute of Personnel and Development, London

Age Diversity in Employment for the Department for Education & Enterprise (DfEE), NOP found that:
- 85% of over-50s believed that there is discrimination against older workers;
- over 95% of employers believed that they had 'age friendly' employment policies and saw no need to change to meet the principles of the Code of Practice;
- 20% of over-50s said that they had had direct experience of age discrimination.

Humberside TEC, The Lottery of Age, 2000:
A Training & Enterprise survey of employers and individuals in the Humberside area concluded, four years after the TEC's first report on age diversity, that 'ageism is rife'.

Continental Research for DfEE, June 2000:
Research for the former Department for Education & Enterprise found that:
- 50% of unemployed people over age 50 said that they had been discriminated against on grounds of age;
- 78% said the barriers made it harder to get jobs;
- 45% of over-45s in early retirement said they would like to work again if there were opportunities.

Carnegie UK Trust report, June 2000:
In *A Decade of Progress and Change*, a report on ten years' activity and action on third age issues by the Carnegie Trust, it was noted that 'much remains to be achieved, with statistical measures still pointing to significant exclusion of older people from the economy and with Labour's pledge on legislation still unfulfilled'.

Institute of Directors (IOD) Report, May 2000:
From a survey sample of 500 IOD members:
- half had workforces with less than 10% over age 50 and 10% had no employees over 50;
- yet two-thirds thought that they had 'age friendly' policies and supported in principle legislation on age diversity.

Nationwide Building Society, March 2000:
Nationwide increased the proportion of over-50s in their workforce from 1.5% to 9% between 1990 and 2000, demonstrating the impact of a proactive employer policy on age diversity.

Office for National Statistics, 1999:
ONS reported in *Social Focus on Older People* that only 1 in 10 of those made redundant over the age of 45 ever return to a job. This compares with 60% of under-45s, who find a new job within 3 months.

European Union, November 1999:
At an EU Employment Conference, it was reported that:
- EU countries with the highest level of over-50s employment had the highest level of youth employment (Scandinavia);
- Countries with the lowest levels of over-50s employment had the lowest levels of youth employment (France, Spain, Germany).

Sheffield Hallam University, 1999:
Research reported in *The Detached Male Workforce* concluded that:
- 750,000 people over age 50 would like to be working, if they thought that there was a relevant opportunity to do so;
- 9 out of 10 people over age 50 who started job-hunting on redundancy gave up within 12 months because of the response they experienced.

Institute of Management, 1997:
In *Breaking the Barriers*, the Institute reported that:
- 44% of a sample of 1,648 managers said that they had experienced age discrimination;
- 55% of the sample of managers said that they had used age as a criterion in recruitment.

Experience overseas
Commenting on the upturn in the percentage of older people working in the US, Professor Glennerster of the London School of Economics and Brookings said: 'One is forced to conclude that the policy changes which the Americans made did actually work.'

Winning the Generation Game
Following extensive consultations and reviews of research in the UK, this Cabinet Office report of March 2000 was accepted by the Government. It contains 75 recommendations designed to:
- change the culture to end ageism and raise the expectations of older people;
- enable and encourage over-50s to stay in work;
- help and encourage displaced workers to re-enter work;
- help older people to make use of their skills and experience for the benefit of the wider community.
- The above information is from the Third Age Employment Network's web site: www.taen.org.uk

© *Third Age Employment Network*

21

The worldwide picture

It is hard to believe that there are three million less males in the UK workforce today than there were thirty years ago. This in an age when we are greater in number, living longer and staying fitter. The figures for women are scarcely changed which would indicate that they are not considered as much a threat and probably because, traditionally, women have a tendency to work short-time and part-time.

An added factor is that the traditional 'job for life' attitude is changing. In the future all of us will have to plan our careers differently, in fact we may have to consider two or even three different careers in a 45-year lifespan. The traditional ways of work that we have always known are coming to an end and with this will come many changes in the way we all, including employers, have to view employment. Still the problems of age discrimination must be solved, and quickly. It remains a worldwide problem. Change, as always, is a slow process

The USA

The most notable international contribution to anti-discrimination has been the enactment of the American ADEA in 1967. After many years of trying to solve age discrimination problems by means of 'voluntary codes' the US Administration adopted law with the Age Discrimination in Employment Act of 1967. A great deal of lobby pressure was put on the US Government at this time by organisations like the Gray Panthers and the American Association of Retired Persons (AARP). Enactment has not been perfect, however. Though you will never hear Americans complain too much, the system could be run better. They all agree that having legislation is far better than not having it.

The British Government has arrogantly attempted to discredit the American experience on numerous occasions. One might reason, however, that if it were so bad, it would have been scrapped many years ago. Though some Americans have voiced disquiet to me personally, they would not swap their system for ours. They say that the law is good; it is the application of that law that is not good. Oddly enough Americans are asking CAADE for campaigning advice.

Canada

Canada is typical of a number of countries in the world which have made an attempt to tackle age discrimination problems through existing employment and human rights law. By and large Canadians approve of their country's efforts but insist that they still want specific anti-discrimination legislation on age. As with any other country we always go by the opinions of the general public. Canadians, like many others, despite wanting more from their own government, are appalled with what we have to tolerate here in the UK.

Australia and New Zealand

Australia and New Zealand are amongst the latest countries to consider and enact legislative protection for their older workers. CAADE's colleagues are in regular touch with these countries and they regularly visit the UK. They report that with the new awareness and legislation over there, older workers are much more upbeat about their future prospects.

The Far East

Japan in particular is close to enacting age discrimination legislation. Though historically their social awareness of ADE is different to ours, campaigners have insisted upon, and have achieved, necessary changes. CAADE was a member of an English group welcoming their campaigners and researchers here in 1998.

In the future all of us will have to plan our careers differently

---

South American, Asian and African nations

Most of the young and developing nations of the world are quite naturally turning to the developed world for legislative guidance and it is also true of general attitudes to ageism, a tendency that they also often learn from us. One of the more developed nations of Africa has recently been in touch with CAADE and a dialogue is being developed.

Europe

Europe generally is moving rapidly towards eliminating most of the problems of ageism. France and Germany are currently reversing trends towards early exit from the workforce by introducing early retirement schemes (discussed elsewhere on the web site). Both Ireland and the Netherlands have now introduced legislation. Sweden, for instance, is a most progressive country with legislation that includes a flexible decade of retirement. Over 75% of Swedish workers aged 55-64 are still in employment – the highest figure in Europe by far – Belgium, Spain, Italy, Finland, Greece and Portugal have all got some degree of legal protection for their older workers. With the new regulations coming in from the European Parliament, all of these countries will easily adapt to general legislation against ADE.

The UK

The UK as usual is dragging its heels. Despite promises made by the Prime Minister, the Government still relies on the goodwill of individual companies. However, the new EU Regulations will change all that and we will have legislation here within the next five years. All the more reason why we should maintain pressure on Parliament. The sooner the better.

● The above information is an extract from CAADE's web site which can be found at www.caade.net

Record number of businesses started by over-50s

Over-50s are starting a record number of new businesses according to a survey from Barclays released today.

Images of rocking chairs and slippers are being consigned to the scrap heap as retirees capitalise on their experience to re-enter the world of work – but on their own terms. Barclays report *Third Age Entrepreneurs – Profiting from Experience* shows that older entrepreneurs are responsible for 50% more business start-ups then 10 years ago, starting an estimated 60,000 new businesses in 2000.

Today's third age entrepreneurs work hard – 49% work an average of 36 hours or more – but also rate holidays, lack of stress and a balance between work and home life more highly than their counterparts starting in business when under 50. Only 27% run the business as the only source of income to the household, with 51% supplementing a pension.

Other key findings were:

- Third age start-ups account for an estimated 15% of all new businesses.
- The average turnover of a business started by a third age entrepreneur is £70,000, compared with a national average of £104,000 for those starting in business aged under 50.
- Third age entrepreneurs are three times more likely to be male than female.
- Nearly 35% of third agers started their business because of retirement, redundancy or dissatisfaction with their previous job.

Mike Rogers, managing director of small business and start-ups, said: 'What we are seeing today is a demographic shift as people who previously thought their working lives were over are choosing to re-enter the work place as their own boss. Their experience and know-

BARCLAYS

ledge will be a valuable driver for the enterprise economy.

'The approach of older entrepreneurs to running their own business differs greatly to those under 50 when starting in business, with the desire to be their own boss or turn a hobby into a career among key motivations. Banks, Government and business support organisations need to be acutely aware of their differing needs and the growing importance of this group to the economy.'

Baroness Greengross, expert in parliament on issues concerning older people, said: 'Too often the images about older people can be negative and stereotypical. But this research shows that, as we begin the 21st century, the future doesn't necessarily just lie with the dot.coms run by the 20-something-year-olds. New businesses run by the over-50s are growing both in number and their economic impact.'

By 2025, more than a third of the UK population will be over 55 – compared with 1 in 4 today. And advances in health care and changing attitudes to growing older mean that expectations about the quality of life for the over-50s have also changed. Whilst some have accumulated sufficient wealth to stop work, others need or want to supplement their pension provision with income from a business to maintain or improve their standard of living.

The report's findings successfully challenge typical stereotypes of older people, with entrepreneurs over 50 more likely to own and use a computer in the course of their business activities (63% for over-50s starting in business compared with 47% for under-50s). There is also evidence to suggest that older business owners are much more likely to have invested time and effort in undertaking research and detailed planning before striking out and going it alone – 43% prepare a business plan versus 28% of their younger counterparts and 37% research competitors compared to 23% of those under 50 when starting in business.

Note

Research undertaken by Continental research on behalf of Barclays between 2 and 12 April 2001 amongst a nationally representative sample of 473 small businesses with a turnover of less than £1 million.

© Barclays Group

Experience necessary

The business case for wisdom

Introduction

The pensions timebomb, inter-generational warfare, an over-burdened health service – for many commentators these are the only noteworthy features of our ageing population. Few have a good word to say about the demographic changes that are yielding unprecedented numbers of older people in our society. Ageing is seen as all about loss – becoming less fit, less adaptable, less able. The wave of pessimism surrounding age in our youth-obsessed culture affects even those who might be expected to take a more positive view; pressure groups for older people focus not on creating a new vision of ageing for the twenty-first century, but on the need to preserve benefit rights for a group they characterise as needy and vulnerable.

Hardly surprising, then, that much of the business world is less than enthusiastic at the prospect of an ageing population. But attitudes towards age are changing – with progressive firms at the forefront of change. Over the next few years, successful businesses will lead the way in reassessing the value of age and revealing our ageing population as an economic resource of enormous value. Developments in our economy

By Charlotte Thorne

are bringing about some fundamental changes in the way that businesses work. Ultimately, older workers stand to gain.

> *Recent figures suggest that the employment rate for the over-50s is increasing faster than the rate for the population as a whole*

As the economy matures it is becoming more demanding. Organisations are demanding more than data, more even than information. The current requirement is for knowledge, but businesses are beginning to understand that knowledge is too narrow a concept to describe what they really need – people who can employ their experience and understanding, their networks and their strategic vision to add value to organisations. What businesses are really after is wisdom. Wise workers are set to become an essential resource for successful organisations, and businesses are increasingly finding that the older workers they previously had written off are the richest source of adaptable and creative labour around.

In some economies, the re-evaluation of age is already happening. US figures suggest that whilst older Americans make up 10 per cent of the nation's workforce they represent 22 per cent of the nation's job growth.

Even more strikingly, recent figures from Australia reveal that in the four years between 1996 and 2000, the economy created 360,000 full-time jobs – a staggering three-quarters of which went to workers aged 45 and over.

Changing demographics, in the UK and elsewhere, are adding impetus to the pursuit of wise workers. Declining birth rates mean that employers are going to have to become more creative if they want to access the knowledge workers they need – and that means abandoning the lazy prejudice of age discrimination. Employers failing to exploit the pool of untapped wisdom to be found in older workers are wasting a resource worth £26 billion a year.

But the evidence is that change is already on its way. Recent figures suggest that the employment rate for the over-50s is increasing faster than the rate for the population as a whole. Some businesses still have some catching up to do – but the stage is set for firms to begin reversing their thinking on age and start attracting back to work the wiser, older worker.

• The above information is from the introduction of the publication *Experience Necessary – the business case for wisdom*, by Charlotte Thorne. ISBN: 1 85835 930 9. Published: 10/2000, £20.00. Information about this publication can be obtained from the Work Foundation's web site: www.workfoundation.com

Add seven years to your working life

People in their 20s and 30s could face working until they are 72 unless they up their pensions savings, new analysis warned today.

A worker making typical contributions into a group pension scheme will either face a dramatic cut in their income at 65 or have to keep working for another seven years, the research found.

The analysis, carried out by the Pensions Policy Institute (PPI), came as union leaders warned that the scrapping of tax credits on dividends for pensions funds and the decline in final salary schemes was creating a 'financial nightmare'.

The PPI research showed that workers who had invested in retirement funds over the past 40 years had benefited from high stock-market returns.

Today's 65-year-olds, if they had started their pensions at 25, could expect a pension income worth two-thirds of their salary at retirement, it found.

But current economic conditions mean a 25-year-old who was starting saving today would have to work for 47 years, not 40, to get the same pension income, meaning they would have to work until the age of 72.

Longer life expectancy could mean that their money would also have to last longer.

The PPI research was based on a typical contribution of 11% into a group pension scheme.

It looked at conditions for members of occupational schemes and did not consider the one in three people in the country who have no private pension provision and will probably have to rely on means-tested benefits.

Meanwhile, the TUC disclosed that the number of workers in final salary pension schemes – considered the best kind of occupational scheme – had fallen by almost two million over the past decade.

Some workers have switched to other schemes, but most had been left without any access to occupational pensions, it said.

The TUC is stepping up a campaign aimed at protecting final salary schemes, following an increase in the number of firms deciding to scrap them or transfer employees to inferior pension arrangements.

The decline would continue unless there was a statutory obligation on employers to contribute to a pension scheme, the TUC warned.

Recent closures of final salary pension schemes by firms including food giant Iceland and accountancy firm Ernst and Young were just the tip of a 'very large iceberg', said TUC general secretary John Monks.

'Over the last decade both employers and the state have been shifting responsibility for pensions provision on to individual employees, many of whom have no idea how poor they will be when they retire.

'Employers must be made to contribute to pension schemes.'

The statistical timebombs

There are what we call 'Fixed Census Statistics' and 'sound-bite statistics'. The difference will become obvious. Let's take the Fixed Census figures. A fixed census is taken every ten years in the UK. There was one due this year (2001). The last census showed up the following:

- By the year 2002 a half of the electorate and a half of the workforce will be over the age of 45. A state of parity.
- Until the year 2020 the population of the UK over the age of 45 will rise significantly.
- At the same time the population under the age of 45 will reduce with equal significance.

Sound-bite statistics on the other hand show up the current sociological imbalances on a current and short-term basis, for instance:

- The UK's unemployment and economic inactivity rates for older workers is currently 37.8% – whilst the rate for the rest of the working population is 26.1%.
- Nearly a third of over-45s are without work (some 2.8 million).
- Older workers in the UK are 25% more likely to be unemployed, or economically inactive, than younger workers.
- Over two and a half million workers – more than a third of those between the ages of 45 and 65 – are officially classed as unemployed and economically inactive.
- There are eight times as many older workers out of work for more than twelve months than younger workers.

Age discrimination is not new. It has been going on for many years. However, in the last decade of the last century it became a vicious tool against the older generation.

- The above information is an extract from CAADE's web site which can be found at www.caade.net

Pension age 'must rise to 67 for all'

Britons should be compelled to work until the age of 67 before they get a state pension if the Government is to meet soaring bills for the elderly, according to one of the country's most influential think-tanks.

Life expectancy has shot up since the birth of the welfare state, with today's couples living, on average, three decades longer than their Victorian forebears. Yet the official retirement age of 60 for women and 65 for men has remained unchanged for half a century.

Raising it for the generation now in their thirties and under would allow the state to provide a decent living for pensioners, the Institute for Public Policy Research will argue in a landmark paper to be published next month.

'Retiring at 67 would still leave an average of around 20 years of retirement for most men and women. Many people could expect to live for most of that period in a reasonably robust state of health,' the paper will say.

'Whether the official retirement age is raised or not, the Government should engage the public in a debate about trends towards early retirement in the context of increased healthy life expectancy.'

By Gaby Hinsliff, Chief Political Correspondent

The controversial proposals, expected to be studied closely in Downing Street, would target the 'Bridget Jones' generation rather than current pensioners.

They will trigger huge controversy among workers brought up to dream of early retirement into a life of leisure rather than spending even longer chained to a desk.

> *'There is a pressing need for a change in attitudes towards the third age. It would be much better if people started thinking about getting older now'*

Workers would still be able to retire early if they had enough private funds to tide them over. But research last week from the Institute for Fiscal Studies warned that shrinking savings returns will put an end to most people's hopes of giving up work while still in their fifties.

The report dismisses the idea of a catastrophic demographic time-bomb as the baby boomer generation hits retirement age, with too few workers paying taxes to support an army of pensioners.

But it admits there will be 'dilemmas' over the growing demand for public spending on pensions, healthcare and nursing homes.

It will argue that the move to 67 for both sexes could be phased in by 2030. Ministers have already announced that by 2020 the retirement ages for both men and women will be equalised at 65, meaning many of today's working women must get used to the idea of staying in their jobs for longer anyway.

'There is a pressing need for a change in attitudes towards the third age,' said Richard Brooks, one of the report's authors. 'It would be much better if people started thinking about getting older now, and what they want to have more of and do less of in future.'

In 1951, the average 60-year-old man could expect to live only into his mid-seventies; by 2030, he can expect to live to 82. Meanwhile more people are going to university and starting work later. That means even if pensionable age was raised to

67, the average person would still have around 40 years of leisure – counting their childhood and retirement – against 45 years at work.

Ministers have already pledged to scrap compulsory retirement ages by 2006, meaning no worker could be forced out at 65 if they were healthy and wanted to stay on. It would also become illegal for firms to stipulate a retirement age in a contract. But many of those who stay on could choose to work part-time.

The Treasury has identified a potential pensions trap for those planning to work into their seventies but who are forced out by health problems.

They may be tempted to opt for lower pension contributions while working, thinking they have longer to save up, only to find that they cannot continue as long as they thought and are left with too little when ill health forces them to retire.

• This article first appeared in *The Observer*, Sunday 10 February, 2002.
© *Guardian Newspapers Limited 2002*

Age Concern highlights pension anxiety

Nearly 70% of people are worried about their retirement income and most do not have confidence that the government will tackle pensioner poverty, a campaign group claimed today.

Age Concern claimed that one in five pensioners already lived in absolute poverty and it warned that many young people faced hardship in old age unless they started saving for their retirement.

The group today launched a Fair Pensions for All campaign to highlight the reality of life for today's pensioners and to call on the government to do more to help them and people retiring in the future.

Research carried out for the group found that around 60% of people are dissatisfied with the government's record on improving income for pensioners, while nearly 70% are apprehensive about what their income will be in retirement.

Age Concern said only half the population below state retirement age was currently saving into a pension.

It warned that young people were particularly likely to face difficulties in retirement, with 43% of 25 to 34-year-olds claiming they could not afford to save into a pension or had not thought about it.

More than half of those questioned said they thought the basic state pension should be big enough to provide a disposable income, and only 6% agreed that it should only contribute towards living expenses.

Gordon Lishman, director general of Age Concern England, said: 'One in five pensioners already lives in absolute poverty.

'We cannot allow future generations of pensioners to be pushed below the breadline, but we are at risk of doing just that unless we act in time. The public consensus has shown that the government needs to provide a joined-up pension policy of which the basic state pension remains the foundation.'

Young people were particularly likely to face difficulties in retirement, with 43% of 25 to 34-year-olds claiming they could not afford to save into a pension or had not thought about it

---

The government also needed to show that it was serious about tackling pensioner poverty by announcing clear targets for its reduction.

The group is calling on the government to increase the basic state pension and to warn young people about the income level they face in retirement if they do not save.

Work and Pensions secretary Alistair Darling said: 'Just uprating the basic state pension for all pensioners would do nothing to tackle pensioner poverty. Around 2m pensioners receiving the minimum income guarantee will be at least £20 a week better off from April. But we are making sure all pensioners share in the rising prosperity of the country. From April, basic state pensions rise by £3 for a single pensioner and £4.80 for a couple.'
© *Guardian Newspapers Limited 2002*

Old and on the scrapheap

Help the Aged exposes age discrimination in the heart of public policy

A ground-breaking report *Age Discrimination in Public Policy*, published by the British Gas Help the Aged Partnership provides detailed evidence that age discrimination lies in the heart of public policy, viewing older people as second-class citizens.

A Help the Aged/NOP poll reveals that half the population (51%) believe this country treats older people as if they're on the scrapheap. Forty-four per cent feel that older people are considered to be a burden on society.

The findings come as the British Gas Help the Aged Partnership launch Scrap it! a UK-wide campaign to expose and challenge age discrimination. It coincides with the final month of the Government's current consultation round on their plans to outlaw discrimination in employment on the grounds of age, sexual orientation and religion.

The report provides evidence that blatant discrimination is in force in health and social care, social security, transport, employment and education:

- Age is used to ration resources in the health service, flying in the face of the right to health care on the basis of need and clinical ability to benefit.
- Local authorities have a financial incentive to encourage older people to go into institutional care rather than provide care in the community. This is forcing older people out of their own homes and into residential care. The upper limit on expenditure for an older person in residential or nursing care can be up to 50% less than that spent on a younger adult.
- Older people are excluded from the job market with a dramatic impact on physical and mental health, and costs to the economy of an estimated £31 billion in lost production.[1]

Indirect discrimination is endemic:

- Older people are major users of public transport. The failure of planners to consider the needs of older people increases their isolation, particularly those living in rural areas.
- Older people are less likely to take up benefits to which they are entitled.

Help the Aged Director of Policy, Paul Cann, commented:

'The insidious scourge of age discrimination blights and restricts the lives of older people. Help the Aged welcomes Government steps to end discrimination, but these will be thwarted if age continues to be an arbitrary way of rationing resources and barring access to vital services.

'As long as older people are viewed as second-class citizens they will receive second-rate care that is damaging, degrading and can have tragic consequences. The outcome of the Government's consultation must be to ensure that the right framework is in place to make legislation work, and to extend it beyond employment.

'The Government concedes that age discrimination exists in the NHS. Now it is shown to be endemic across public institutions. There must be a root-and-branch review of public policy, backed up by adequate legislation, to give older people a fair choice and a fair deal.'

Help the Aged believes that voluntary codes are inadequate. It is calling for the legislation on age diversity required by the European Equal Treatment Directive for 2006 to be brought forward and extended to cover goods, services and facilities. Legislation must be supported by a commission to ensure its enforcement and promote equality for older people.

Reference

1. Ricard, S (2001) *Ageism – Too Costly to Ignore*, Cranfield School of Management for the Employers' Forum on Age. May 2001.

- The report *Age Discrimination in Public Policy* was written by contributors who are experts in their field. They were Patrick Grattan – employment; Brian Groombridge – citizenship; Melanie Henwood – social services; Marilyn Howard – social security; David Metz – transport; Emilie Roberts – health; and Jim Soulsby – education. The foreword was written by Margaret Simey, a retired social scientist.

- Copies of the full report are available at £18.50 inc. post and packing from Help the Aged Communications Department, 207-221 Pentonville Road, London, N1 9UZ. A summary is available on the Help the Aged web site.

- The above information is from Help the Aged's web site which can be found at www.helptheaged.org.uk

© Help the Aged

Ageing

Ageing affects us all, so most of us have questions about it. This article answers the questions we are most often asked. You may find some of the answers surprising – we hope you will find them interesting and useful

What is ageing?

Ageing is a natural process that affects most, but not all, living things. We used to believe that ageing was programmed into us by some kind of biological clock, but that view is no longer widely held. It is now thought that ageing is the result of accumulated damage to the cells and tissues of our bodies; over time, microscopic faults impair normal functioning and may lead to disease. If we can understand cell ageing and find ways of reducing the accumulation of cell damage, or increase the effectiveness of our repair mechanisms, we might be able to delay the onset of disease and improve the quality of old age.

The kinds of damage most likely to cause age-associated or degenerative disease are in the genetic material (DNA) of cells and the accumulation of altered components within cells. Altered cell proteins are implicated in the development of diseases as diverse as Alzheimer's disease and cataracts, while DNA mutations play a part in cancers and in muscle weakness.

Much of this cellular damage arises as a by-product of normal living. For example, some of the oxygen we breathe gives rise to highly reactive molecules called free radicals which can damage DNA and proteins. Our bodies have excellent natural defence mechanisms against these free radicals, which is why we live as long as we do, but some faults slip through.

Although much research has been and is being done on ageing, there is still much we do not know. Ageing is an exciting and fascinating field of study for scientists in disciplines as diverse as molecular biology, nutrition, medicine, neuro-science, psychiatry and genetics.

Why have our lifespans increased?

In the twentieth century average lifespans increased by over 20 years in the UK and many other developed countries, and our lifespans are continuing to increase. Many factors have contributed to this phenomenal success story.

Higher living standards have played a key role. Today we have better diets than our relatives of a century ago, with the result that our immune systems are in better shape to withstand infections like bronchitis and influenza that previously caused many early deaths. We no longer live in over-crowded, damp or unsanitary housing where disease was common and easily spread.

We now have safe, clean drinking water, proper sanitation and much higher standards of hygiene in public places and the home. These measures have helped eliminate preventable illnesses like typhoid, cholera and dysentery. Although air pollution is still a major health issue, our air is much cleaner than it was a century ago when factory chimneys and domestic fires belched smoke and gave rise to chronic chest problems in a high proportion of the population.

Medical science has also made a major contribution. The twentieth century saw the big breakthroughs in vaccination and immunisation, with the result that killer diseases like diphtheria, tuberculosis and polio were held in check. Smallpox became the first disease to be eliminated altogether by an international programme of vaccination. The development of antibiotics gave the first effective treatment against other serious infections, enabling people to survive illnesses like pneumonia. Better medical care has also meant that few women now die in childbirth and it has dramatically improved the life chances of small or premature babies.

The significance of all these advances is that they have enabled more people than ever before to survive the rigours of childhood and young adulthood. Of a million babies born in England and Wales in the 1880s, more than a quarter (263,000) died before their fifth birthday, and just over half were still alive at 35. It was these early deaths that kept average life expectancy so low. Of a million babies born in the 1990s, more than four-fifths (831,000) will still be alive at 65, so average life expectancy is much higher.

Why do women live longer than men?

Women do indeed live longer than men in most countries of the world. In the UK, life expectancy, at birth, is 74 for men, whereas it is 81 for women, a difference of seven years. The figures for other developed countries are broadly similar. In a few countries, like Bangladesh for instance, men live slightly longer than women (with a life expectancy of 57 and 56 respectively), but such places are now the exception. The reason women have shorter lives in countries like Bangladesh is due to the lack of investment in women's health and particularly in maternal health.

There are two answers to the puzzle as to why women last the distance better than men do. Lifestyle

Although much research has been and is being done on ageing, there is still much we do not know. Ageing is an exciting and fascinating field of study

plays a very important role in our life expectancy, and men often make unhealthy choices. Men are more likely than women to smoke, with the result that more die before their time of lung cancer, other smoking-related cancers, and heart disease. Excessive intake of alcohol is a factor in men's premature deaths in some societies, while in many industrialised countries deaths from occupational causes inflict a greater toll on men than on women. It may also be true that women are physically more active throughout life; women do more of the 'physiotherapy of daily living', such as getting the shopping in and doing the housework, and exercise protects against many age-related conditions.

But there are also biological answers. There is growing evidence that women are biologically tougher than men. For example, we now know that female hormones protect women from heart disease, at least until the menopause. The reasons for women's biological resilience have to do with the way we have all evolved to play our reproductive roles. Put simply, we have evolved to reproduce and pass our genes on to future generations. Our genes stand a better chance of survival if the nurturing parent – the mother – survives to care for her offspring until they are able to fend for themselves. In biological terms, men are expendable at younger ages because their genetic investment does not depend on their personal survival.

How healthy are older people in the UK?

This is a surprisingly difficult question to answer due to a shortage of national information on our state of health. We do know a great deal about the prevalence of specific disorders; stroke, for example, becomes more common with age. Three out of four strokes occur in people over the age of 65, and the incidence rises with increasing age.

However, it is easy from these studies to view older generations as unhealthy and even downright decrepit. The truth is more complex. The General Household Survey, carried out by the Office for National Statistics, asks some helpful questions about the ability of people over 65 to do basic tasks, from which we know that:

- 91 per cent can get around the house with no difficulty;
- 72 per cent can get up and down stairs with no difficulty;
- 77 per cent can get out and about on their own with no difficulty.

These figures imply a fairly fit and active older population. We also know from studies of particular diseases that most older people enjoy good mental health too. To turn the usual statistics on their heads:

- 95 per cent of people aged between 70-80 are unaffected by dementia;
- 80 per cent of those aged 80-90 do not have dementia;
- 66 per cent of those aged 90 plus are free of dementia;
- 85-90 per cent of people over 65 do not suffer from depression.

What the statistics do show is a considerable difference between the health of 'young elderly' people in their 60s, and that of their own parents' generation in their 80s and 90s. 'Young elderly' people are remarkably fit; many of our business leaders, politicians, entertainers and writers belong to this cohort, as do a high proportion of users of the Internet! Their parents are the generation most at risk of age-related conditions like heart disease, stroke, cancer, arthritis, dementia, and disabling sensory losses, especially deafness but also impaired sight. The good news is that illness and disability tend to be compressed into a few short years at the end of our long lives, and one of the aims of Research into Ageing is to reduce this period still further.

Will older people be fitter in the future?

In all probability, yes. It is difficult to look to the future with total certainty. Current trends towards healthier lives may be blown off course by unpredictable factors such as major economic recession (there is a powerful link between poverty and ill health) or the fashion for smoking, to give just two examples. The numbers of people who smoke have been in steady decline in the past decades, but if that single trend were to be reversed, we could expect to see a worsening of the nation's health.

But with these provisos in mind, the future does look very promising. First, there is considerable scope to prevent some of the disabling conditions of later life. Stroke and osteoporosis (thinning of the bones) are two good examples. Stroke can be prevented by controlling blood pressure and reducing smoking. Osteoporosis affects women more commonly than men and can be held in check by hormone replacement therapy, exercise and higher intake of calcium and vitamin D.

Second, there is every likelihood that the next few decades will see major break-throughs in treating some common conditions. There is currently no treatment for

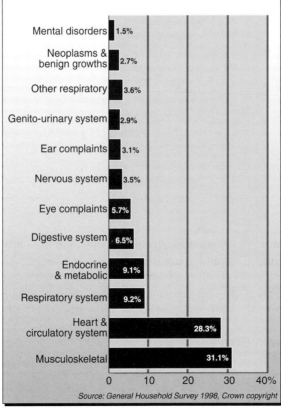

Longstanding conditions

The most common longstanding conditions reported by people over 65

Condition	Percentage
Mental disorders	1.5%
Neoplasms & benign growths	2.7%
Other respiratory	3.6%
Genito-urinary system	2.9%
Ear complaints	3.1%
Nervous system	3.5%
Eye complaints	5.7%
Digestive system	6.5%
Endocrine & metabolic	9.1%
Respiratory system	9.2%
Heart & circulatory system	28.3%
Musculoskeletal	31.1%

Source: General Household Survey 1998, Crown copyright

stroke, though careful management of the condition in special stroke units dramatically increases the chance of survival. But the race is on to find effective treatments for stroke, some of them funded by Research into Ageing, and the next decade may produce real advances. Sound biomedical research is likely to yield similar dividends for conditions as diverse as heart disease, some cancers and Alzheimer's disease.

Third, we are on the brink of unravelling the human gene code. This understanding will undoubtedly pave the way for further advances in the prevention and treatment of many illnesses.

Whatever the outcomes of science, our future health is, to a large extent, in our own hands. Most preventive strategies will only work if we are receptive to health messages. A healthy lifestyle is a prerequisite for a healthier old age – which brings us to the next question.

What is the best way to stay healthy in later life?

Thanks to decades of biomedical research, there are some clear pointers as to how to stay fit and well throughout later life. Our lifestyle accounts for the most significant 'slice' of our chances of ageing successfully (our genes make up only a 25-33 per cent slice), and lifestyle is something about which we can all make choices.

Smoking is the biggest single health risk any of us takes. Smokers have shorter lives due to lung cancer, cancer of the bladder, mouth and other organs, heart disease, bronchi-

tis, asthma and other conditions. It is by no means easy to give up smoking, but doing so gives immediate benefits, no matter how old you are or how long you have been a smoker.

A good diet is vital to good health. Our food does not just provide the energy we need for daily living, it also provides the raw materials for healthy cell turnover and fuels our natural repair system. A healthy diet includes:

- at least five portions of fruit and vegetables a day. These provide the anti-oxidant vitamins that protect us against the ravages of free radicals as well as other nutrients and fibre. Fruit and vegetables can protect us from developing most of the chronic diseases we associate with later life;
- starches and fibre such as potatoes, rice, wholemeal bread and pasta. These are energy-giving foods, but also provide essential B vitamins and dietary fibre;
- lean meat, fish, nuts, pulses, eggs and cheese provide the proteins we need for growth and repair. In later life we do not need the large amounts of protein that children and young people need, but we still need daily helpings;
- the right fats. Unsaturated fats such as vegetable oils are healthier than saturated fats such as butter, but all fats should be used sparingly;
- the right fluids in the right quantities. Copious quantities of water and fruit juices will keep

our fluid balance right. Alcohol in moderation, and especially red wine, is also beneficial;
- salt and sugars should be taken in moderation.

Being overweight will seriously reduce the chances of a healthy older age as there is a greater risk of heart disease, stroke, arthritis and diabetes. If you have a weight problem, talk to your doctor about ways to tackle it.

Regular exercise helps to prevent high blood pressure, heart disease, stroke, poor circulation, depression, obesity, joint and bone problems – in fact a very long list of the ailments of later life! An enjoyable form of activity, be it walking, cycling, swimming, dancing or whatever, undertaken for three or four 20-minute sessions a week, can make the difference between good health and sickness and immobility. The right exercise not only keeps us healthy, it enhances general enjoyment of life because it puts the vitality into our years. Older people are advised to take medical advice before starting unaccustomed exercise, however, and it is always a good idea to build up exercise tolerance gradually.

The brain needs exercise too, as research shows that our cognitive functions can be kept agile by doing regular mental gymnastics. Crosswords and puzzles are excellent mental gyms, as are discussion groups and many kinds of voluntary work. Learning something new is a good way to exercise the brain and we are never too old to learn a new skill, whether it is how to use a computer and go surfing the Internet, or a new language, or a craft skill. Developing new interests in later life is also a good strategy for avoiding depression.

The best time to adopt a healthy lifestyle is when we are young – it is, after all, an investment in our own future. But it's never too late to start. Our exercise research has shown that people in their 80s and 90s can regain muscle strength and mobility by regular gentle exercises.

• The above information is an extract from Research into Ageing's web site which can be found at www.ageing.org

© Research into Ageing

Health crisis looms as life expectancy soars

Average ageing forecasts far too low, say scientists

Western governments are drastically underestimating how long their citizens are likely to live, an oversight which threatens to put strains on the health, welfare and pensions systems of the developed world far more serious than previously envisaged, scientists warn today.

Until recently, the growing awareness that governments were, unwittingly, living a lie over life expectancy was largely confined to a small circle of specialist demographers. But the latest high-profile critique of scientific complacency on increasing average lifespans will be hard to ignore.

For years, scientists have been advising governments that the astonishing increases in life expectancy over the past century, which saw typical British male lifespans go from 48 in 1901 to 75 in 2000 and female from 49 to 80, will not continue.

But in the journal *Science* today, two scientists from Cambridge and Rostock in Germany say there is every reason to think that life expectancy will go on increasing indefinitely.

By comparing differences in life expectancy between the world's wealthier countries, they conclude that as early as 2070, female life expectancy in the US could be as high as 101 years. The official US forecast for 2070 is only 83.9 years.

One of the scientists, James Vaupel of the Max Planck Institute for Demographic Research in Rostock, believes that a typical female baby born this year in France or Japan – the two countries with the greatest life expectancy – already has a 50/50 chance of living to be 100.

The *Science* paper gives no estimates for Britain. But using the same methodology, female life expectancy in Japan would reach 100

By James Meek, Science Correspondent

in 2060, with Britain following in 2085.

If true, the study has implications not just for pensions but for healthcare and social services, since there is no guarantee that average healthspan – the time people are free of chronic illness – will keep pace with average lifespan.

Government figures show that for men life expectancy went up from 70.9 to 74.6 between 1981 and 1997, but healthy life expectancy went up from 64.4 to 66.9. In women, the healthy life expectancy increase lagged a year behind life expectancy.

Last night Frank Field, Labour MP for Birkenhead and chairman of parliament's all-party committee on pensions, welcomed the report and called for an independent body to be set up, like the monetary policy committee which sets interest rates, to fix increased retirement ages.

'If you look at life expectancy in 1948, when the state pension was introduced, and take that as a

reasonable length of time to receive a pension, you would have a retirement age of 74 today,' he said.

On Wednesday the UK insurance firm AXA called for the retirement age to be raised to 70.

Dr Vaupel's co-author Jim Oeppen, of Cambridge University's Group for the History of Population and Social Structure, told the *Guardian* that at the moment the government predicts British male life expectancy will rise from 75 to 79 and female from 80 to 83 by 2025. Yet both these levels have already been reached by Japan.

'So the government thinks we're only going to catch up with Japan's present position in 25 years' time. That seems pessimistic to me,' he said.

'We have to strongly consider that current forecasts of the elderly are actually too low. Not only will the numbers be greater, but there will be more at the older end of the scale.'

In their paper, Oeppen and Vaupel describe the relentlessness of the increase in longevity since 1840 as 'the most remarkable regularity of mass endeavour ever observed'.

'Reductions in mortality should not be seen as a disconnected sequence of unrepeatable revolutions but rather as a regular stream of continuing progress... The details are complicated but the resultant straight line of life expectancy increase is simple.'

Life expectancy is not the same as maximum lifespan, which is the oldest any human being has been proved to live, currently 122. Life expectancy is an average. In the 1880s many lived to their 60s and 70s, but almost a quarter of those born died before they were five, bringing down the average.

During the 20th century, a succession of scientists declared absolute limits to life expectancy. In 1928, the US demographer Louis Dublin said it was unlikely to exceed 64.75 years. However, non-Maori New Zealand women already had a life expectancy of 66.

In 1990, Dublin's successors said that without fundamental breakthroughs in controlling ageing itself, 50-year-olds could not expect to live longer than 35 more years. Six years later, Japanese women went through that barrier.

'The ignominious saga of life expectancy maxima is more than an exquisite case for historians intrigued by the foibles of science,' write Oeppen and Vaupel. 'Continuing belief in imminent limits is distorting public and private decision making.

'The officials responsible for making projections have recalcitrantly assumed that life expectancy will increase slowly and not much further. The official forecasts distort people's decisions about how much to save and when to retire. They give politicians licence to postpone painful adjustments to social security and medical care systems.'

The paper accuses colleagues of using 'empirical misconceptions and specious theories' to reassure policy-makers.

Professor Alan Walker of Sheffield University, director of the Economic and Social Research Council's growing old programme, said the paper's conclusions were not news to him but, with the possible exception of Germany, were not yet being faced up to by governments. 'They're right in saying there has been – not a conspiracy, but almost a self-fulfilling prophecy among demographers, where you self-cite your own work and call up your own consensus that life expectancy is finite, but it's not well founded,' he said.

'Policy-makers are now just beginning to recognise the potential significance of increased life expectancy. It's not clear to me that the British policy-making process has fully adapted to this sort of finding, and it has to.'

Elderly 'missing out on basic care'

By Sarah Boseley

The lives of up to 1m elderly people are being put at risk because they are not getting basic care and support at home and there are too few places in residential care, according to a report.

Only the most desperate and needy asked for help from social services, said Help the Aged, one of 21 organisations that have contributed to the report. 'They use social services as an emergency measure,' said a spokeswoman, Hilary Carter.

Yet the services they needed were seriously stretched because of underfunding, leaving many without help to carry on their daily lives. 'When they do not have access to social care, lives are put at risk,' Ms Carter said.

The Social Policy Ageing and Information Network report has been written and led by Help the Aged, Centre for Policy on Ageing, Arthritis Care, Age Concern and Alzheimer's Society.

It said that just over 1m elderly people, most in their 80s or older, received some sort of social care – about half in their own homes and half in residential homes. Many were disabled and a high proportion suffered from mental health conditions such as dementia.

The most visible consequence of the shortfall in funding was probably in hospitals. There was a shortage of suitable care homes for elderly people who were admitted to hospital but could no longer cope in their own homes when discharged. Nearly 700,000 suffered delays in their discharge every year, the report said.

The government has promised an extra £300m over two years to sort out the delays, but the report is pessimistic that the money will have much effect. 'It is not clear how far this money will go to resolve this problem, nor what proportion is likely to be spent on social care.

'The new money is geared to tackle only the most visible tip of the iceberg – older people occupying a bed who need alternative care. Others are waiting out of sight in their own homes and many of those who are helped to leave hospital will need long-term support.'

The half a million living in their own homes needed regular visits, often more than once a day, to help with the most basic of tasks such as getting in and out of bed, getting dressed and keeping clean.

Increasingly, social care was providing what used to be nursing care, such as changing dressings and treating pressure sores. Often there was no time to enhance the lives of these elderly people by helping them get out or keep in touch with family and friends.

Neil Betteridge, of Arthritis Care, said: 'The report is a shocking indictment of how so many vulnerable people are having their basic civil and human rights eroded.'

Gillian Dalley, director of the Centre for Policy on Ageing, said: 'Many of the valuable targets to improve the quality of older people's care in the NHS plan and the national service framework will fall by the wayside if this imbalance in funding between health and social care is not addressed.'

Healthy old age is myth for many

Information from MORI

A new MORI survey shows that many millions of British people have unrealistic expectations of a healthy old age.

The survey commissioned by the recently merged charities Help the Aged and Research into Ageing shows that 68 per cent of people expect to be fit and healthy in old age. However, the reality is that at least two-thirds of people over the age of 75 have a long-standing illness and that 50 per cent of the population over the age of 75 say their illness limits them from leading a full and active life.*

And although we are all living for longer, health trends predict that people born in Britain today will experience longer periods of ill health than any other generation.**

But support for medical research into the illnesses affecting people in old age is still not viewed as a priority by the general public. The MORI poll asked 1,979 respondents across the UK to name the two or three forms of medical research most deserving of additional financial support. Cancer came top (81 per cent), followed by heart disease (52 per cent) and children's illnesses such as asthma and leukaemia (50 per cent).

Only 20 per cent of respondents believed that research into illnesses which affect people in old age, such as arthritis or dementia, should be made a priority and given additional financial support.

Help the Aged Director-General Michael Lake said: 'While many people want to enjoy a full and active retirement, the far from comforting truth is that many of us will have a debilitating illness in old age. Poorer health means financial hardship and isolation for many older people.

'The importance of medical research in this area grows ever more pressing to improve our chances of a healthy and independent old age. Help the Aged has merged with and will be funding the charity Research into Ageing precisely to tackle ill health in old age.'

The survey assessed people's positive and negative attitudes towards growing old. When asked to identify the two or three good things about growing old, people said they looked forward to an old age which was both active and sociable, with 44 per cent of people naming more time for hobbies and leisure, 41 per cent wanting to spend more time with family and friends, and 37 per cent identifying more time for holidays and travel.

But when asked about their two or three greatest worries about growing old, 44 per cent of respondents said they feared losing their mobility and 34 per cent said they worried about losing friends and family through death.

Caroline Bradley from Research into Ageing said, 'It is good to see high expectations of a healthy old age. The reality will sadly be very different for too many of us. High-quality scientific research can do a lot to reduce the likelihood of common conditions like osteoporosis, stroke and mobility and funding more biomedical research now is vital to improve the quality of our later lives.'

Notes

Help the Aged merged with Research into Ageing in May 2001. Help the Aged is to match Research into Ageing's £1 million spend this year on clinical and biomedical research, with a further £1 million pledged for 2002. Research into Ageing will continue to raise funds earmarked for medical research.

Research into Ageing funds research into the most common illnesses affecting old age, including mobility, dementia, bone disease, wound healing, stroke and heart disease.

* Source: *General Household Survey* 1998; Table 7.1 Trends in self-reported sickness by sex and age.

** Source: ONS *Health Statistics Quarterly* 2000. 'Life expectancy has increased at a faster rate than healthy life expectancy, with the result that the proportion of life that people can expect to spend in poor health has also increased.'

• The above information is from MORI's web site which can be found at www.mori.com

© MORI (Market & Opinion Research International Limited)

Turning your back on us

There is overwhelming evidence that the NHS discriminates against older people

An Age Concern/Gallup survey showed that one in 20 people over 65 has been refused treatment, while one in ten has been treated differently since the age of 50.

Older people report discrimination at all levels of the health service, from primary care through to hospitals. It is often explicit, such as when patients are told that a treatment is unavailable to them because of their age. This includes 40 per cent of coronary care units attaching age restrictions to the use of clot-busting drug therapy, the refusal of kidney dialysis or transplants to 66 per cent of kidney patients aged 70 to 79.4 and no invitations to breast screening for women aged 65 and over.

The discrimination can also be implicit, such as when older people are given a low priority by the NHS or experience poor levels of care. This includes delays in hip replacements, the withdrawal of chiropody services which makes many older people housebound, and the often inappropriate use of anti-psychotic drugs in care homes. Many older people also report negative attitudes from NHS staff, which can deny them access to services and the quality of care expected by younger people.

In summary, this report concludes that:

- Despite Government assurances of equal treatment, discrimination against older people is widespread within the NHS.

  Example: Joyce Morgan is a former nurse, diagnostic radiographer and social worker, 'I have met too many old people who almost apologise for being alive . . . Old people are not being treated as equals. They just seem to be in the way.'

- The Government and NHS appear to remain unaware of the extent to which age discrimination exists within the health service.

  Example: Linda Wells was horrified at the treatment of elderly patients in hospital, 'It wouldn't take much to change these things – only a better attitude and a little common sense. But if no one stops them happening, they will spread.'

- There is evidence of national and local policies which use age as a barrier to receiving health services.

  Example: Leonard Wilson has been told that because he is over 60, he will not be given a new heart. 'If I had become ill at 59, would I have been treated? . . . We hear that life expectancy for men is 85. That's another 20 years from where I am now.'

- The Government states that older people can expect to be well nourished, clean, comfortable and treated with respect. But there is evidence of a failure to provide these essentials of care.

  Example: When Lynne Murrell visited her father in hospital, she found him lying on a mattress on the floor with no bedclothes. Then a nurse put a message above his bed to warn staff that he had been 'troublesome'. Lynne says, 'I am disgusted that the NHS tolerates this sort of behaviour. Quite frankly, this nurse did not deserve the privilege of nursing him.'

- Older people are often unwilling to complain when things go wrong, for fear of reprisals or further discrimination.

  Example: Parris Perry explains how she spoke out about unfair treatment. But she says, 'Many people of my generation see doctors as gods and would never contradict them. Or they're just frightened.'

- Where a complaint is against a GP, many older people fear that they will be removed from the GP's list.

  Example: An anonymous account reports discrimination, but describes the fear of speaking out, 'I have heard of so many instances of patients being "struck off" a GP's list

for no other reason than that the senior GP does not like them.'

- Many NHS staff are insensitive to the needs of older people. Their attitude is often described as dismissive and disrespectful.

  Example: Lorraine Hughes explains, 'My father's perception is that he is treated as "an old fuddy duddy" who is past thinking for himself . . . and he is not worthy of respectful treatment.' She describes a 'double discrimination' of ageism and racism in the treatment of him.

- There is insufficient emphasis on promoting and safeguarding the quality of life of older people.

  Example: Terry Cammack argues that, without his support, his father would not have got the operation he needed. 'My father was losing his mobility, finding it more difficult to look after himself and his morale was being affected . . . If he hadn't had the operation, he would almost certainly have gone into a home.'

Age Concern is calling on the Government to carry out a thorough investigation of age discrimination in the NHS.

- The above information is the executive summary from *Turning your back on us*, a report by Age Concern. See page 41 for their address details or visit their web site at www.ageconcern.org.uk

© 2002 Age Concern England

35

Dementia

Information from the Alzheimer's Society

What is dementia?

The term 'dementia' describes a group of symptoms caused by the impact of disease on the brain.

While each person is unique and will experience dementia in their own way, symptoms typically include problems with memory, speech and perception.

Short-term memory is usually affected. This may mean, for example, that the person with dementia forgets the names of family or friends, or how to perform simple everyday tasks. They may, however, retain their long-term memory, clearly remembering events from the past.

The person with dementia might have problems finding the right words, or may seem to have difficulties understanding what is being said to them. As verbal communication diminishes, they may retain the ability to communicate feelings, needs and preferences through facial expression and body language.

Perception is also usually affected, as the person with dementia tries to interpret and make sense of the world about them. This may make their behaviour and speech appear different to those of other people.

Alzheimer's
Dementia care & research

What causes dementia?

Alzheimer's disease

Alzheimer's disease is the most common cause of dementia. During the course of the disease the chemistry of the brain changes and cells, nerves and transmitters are attacked. Eventually the brain shrinks as gaps develop. After death

---

While each person is unique and will experience dementia in their own way, symptoms typically include problems with memory, speech and perception

---

tangles and plaques made from protein fragments, dying cells and nerve ends can be observed in brain tissue.

The disease typically begins with lapses in memory, mood swings, and difficulty finding the right words. Later the person affected may become more confused and may find it difficult to understand what is being said.

Vascular dementia

Vascular dementia describes all those forms of dementia caused by damage to the blood vessels leading to the brain. The brain relies on a network of vessels to bring it oxygen-bearing blood. If the oxygen supply to the brain fails, brain cells are likely to die. Symptoms of vascular dementia can either happen suddenly following a stroke, or over time through a series of small strokes in the brain, known as multi-infarct dementia. In vascular dementia some mental abilities may be unchanged. The person affected may also have some insight into their own condition. Symptoms may include depression or mood swings.

Dementia with Lewy bodies

This form of dementia gets its name

Alzheimer's

There are over half a million people with Alzheimer's in the UK today. This figure is predicted to double within the next twenty years. There is no cure, long-term treatment or prevention for Alzheimer's.

Why urgent research is needed. Annual UK research spend

	Per patient	Total (millions)
Cancer	£289	£188.5
Stroke	£79	£9.8
Heart disease	£28	£58.4
Alzheimer's	**£11**	**£5.5**

The cost of care for Alzheimer's is more than the other three major diseases put together

	Per patient	Total (millions)
Cancer	£1	655,000
Stroke	£3	124,000
Heart disease	£4	2,053,000
Alzheimer's	**£11**	**527,000**

Source: Alzheimer's Research Trust

from the tiny spherical structures made of proteins that develop inside nerve cells. Their presence in the brain leads to the degeneration and death of brain tissue, affecting memory, concentration and language skills. People with dementia with Lewy bodies may have visual hallucinations. They may also develop physical problems such as slowness of movement, stiffness and tremor.

Other forms of dementia

There are other less common causes of dementia. These include:

- Degenerative conditions. In Pick's disease, for example, damage to brain cells is more localised than in Alzheimer's disease, usually beginning in the front part of the brain, or frontal lobe. Initially personality and behaviour are more affected than memory, but in the later stages symptoms are similar to those of Alzheimer's disease.
- Infection. Prion diseases, for example, which include Creutzfeldt-Jakob disease (CJD), are caused by infectious agents called prions which attack brain tissue. The variant form of the disease (vCJD) has been linked to BSE, a prion disease affecting cattle. The number of cases of vCJD remains low.

People with the AIDS virus can also have dementia, typically in the later stages of the illness.

- Dementia can also be caused by the effect of toxins on the brain. General alcohol dementia is characterised by damage throughout the brain. Wernicke's encephalopathy and Korsakoff's syndrome are also caused by the abuse of alcohol, but the damage to the brain is more specific, particularly occurring in the frontal lobes.
- Finally, those people who have had a head injury with loss of consciousness may be more likely to develop dementia.

Dementia-like symptoms may also be caused by treatable conditions, such as severe depression, urinary infection, vitamin deficiency and brain tumour. For this reason it is important to get an early diagnosis.

Statistics on dementia

The Alzheimer's Society estimates that there are currently over 700,000 people in the UK with dementia.

Regionally, this figure can be broken down:

England	634,000
Scotland	60,600
Northern Ireland	14,900
Wales	40,600
Total	750,100

These numbers are expected to rise gradually over the next 25 years or so as the population ages. This steady increase reflects the worldwide picture of dementia.

There are currently nearly 18 million people with dementia in the world. This is set to rise to around 34 million by 2025. Of this total, 71 per cent will be living in developing countries.

Who gets dementia?

Dementia primarily affects older people. While it is estimated that there are around 18,500 people under the age of 65 with dementia in the UK, the chances of having the condition rise sharply with age.

One in 20 people over the age of 65 will develop dementia. This compares to 1 in 5 people over the age of 80.

But dementia is not an inevitable consequence of old age. Most 90-year-olds, for example, do not have the condition.

What type of dementia is most common?

Determining the incidence of each of the different types of dementia is not a straightforward task.

It may not always be possible to get an accurate diagnosis during life. A final diagnosis may only be given after death when changes to the structure of the brain can be directly observed. And it is also possible to have more than one form of dementia. For example, people with vascular dementia may have some of the symptoms of Alzheimer's disease.

Despite these problems, it is generally agreed that the proportion of those with different forms of dementia can be broken down:

Alzheimer's disease	55%
Vascular dementia	20%
Dementia with Lewy bodies	15%
Pick's disease and frontal lobe dementia	5%
Other dementias	5%

• The above information is an extract from the Alzheimer's Society's web site which can be found at www.alzheimers.org.uk

© *Alzheimer's Society*

Alzheimer's cases in UK 'will double in 40 years'

By Tim Utton,
Science Reporter

The number of people suffering from Alzheimer's disease in the UK will double over the next 40 years, reveals a survey.

Currently, the degenerative brain disorder affects about 700,000 Britons. As the population ages, the figure will rise to 1.5 million.

The study shows that globally one in ten people aged over 60 currently has the disease.

But fewer than half receive treatment because they think nothing can be done for them.

In fact, drugs are available to 'help ease the burden'.

Worldwide, the incidence of the disease would triple to 34 million sufferers between now and 2040 with the biggest increases in India and China, researchers predicted. Ben Greener, neurology analyst at analysts Datamonitor, who produced the survey, said: 'Whilst there is no cure for Alzheimer's, there are drugs that can help modify its progress and effectively reduce the burden of the disease for the sufferers and their families.

'These drugs all work in much the same way – by prolonging the action of a vital neurotransmitter, a chemical that transmits impulses between nerve cells in the brain that is depleted in Alzheimer's sufferers.'

The disease develops in stages, gradually destroying memory, reason, judgement and language – and eventually the ability to carry out even the simplest of tasks.

It is the most widespread form of dementia and although sufferers can be under 40, most are over 60.

A total of 220 doctors worldwide were questioned for the Datamonitor survey. They reported that a huge number of patients did not seek diagnosis of their symptoms, 'mistakenly believing it is just an unpleasant side-effect of old age'.

The neurologists said although the exact cause of Alzheimer's was still unclear, early treatment was vital.

Studies have shown that drugs are far more effective in the initial stages of the disease, and can greatly improve the quality of life for both patients and carers.

> *Worldwide, the incidence of the disease would triple to 34 million sufferers between now and 2040 with the biggest increases in India and China*

The report said a rise in early diagnosis rates would depend on increased public awareness of the disease and the treatments available, as well as the introduction of more accurate and efficient tests.

Mr Greener added: 'In the face of a rise in patient numbers, the biggest challenge will be for governments to improve support and quality of life with non-pharmacological methods for both the patient and carer groups, whilst controlling healthcare spending.'

Dr Richard Harvey, director of research for the Alzheimer's Society, said: 'Increasing life expectancy will lead to more people with Alzheimer's and other forms of dementia.

'For such a serious and damaging disease, it is a scandal that less than half of people with dementia seek a diagnosis, and that only one in three received any form of treatment.

'Investigation and diagnosis is critical to ensuring that the major, life-destroying symptoms of dementia are not due to a treatable illness.'

He added: 'Having a diagnosis of Alzheimer's also helps people get the help they need through organisations such as the society.

'Empowering people with dementia and their carers to seek a diagnosis and request treatment as early as possible is critically important.'

© The Daily Mail
April, 2002

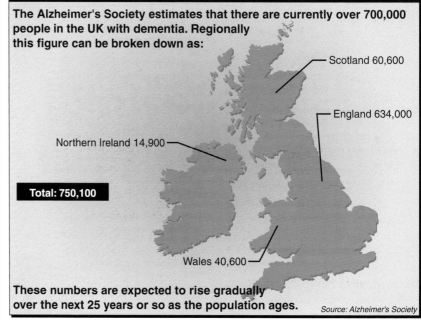

Statistics on dementia

The Alzheimer's Society estimates that there are currently over 700,000 people in the UK with dementia. Regionally this figure can be broken down as:

Scotland 60,600

England 634,000

Northern Ireland 14,900

Wales 40,600

Total: 750,100

These numbers are expected to rise gradually over the next 25 years or so as the population ages. *Source: Alzheimer's Society*

Forget me not 2002

Developing mental health services for older people in England

orget Me Not, published in January 2000, set out the Audit Commission's analysis of mental health services for older people in England and Wales. Since then auditors appointed by the Commission have been carrying out local audits of these services. This report summarises the main findings from audits in England. It highlights for managers and practitioners where they should concentrate their efforts.

Many GPs need more support . . .
- Two-fifths were reluctant to diagnose dementia early.
- The majority did not use protocols to help diagnose dementia or depression.
- Over a third felt they did not have ready access to specialist advice.
- Less than half felt they had received sufficient training for dementia.

. . . but specialist support and training for them can be limited
- It was comprehensive in only 15 per cent of areas.
- It was not available at all in 40 per cent of areas.

Carers of people with dementia need good advice and information
- Nearly all were told what was wrong with their relative.
- Two-thirds were told how things would develop.
- But three-quarters of areas lacked good written information about local services.

Specialist services need strengthening in some areas . . .
- Specialist teams for older people with mental health problems were fully available in less than half of all areas, although were partly available in a further third.
- They often did not have all the recommended core team members.

. . . with more day and respite care
- Day hospitals provided comprehensive assessment and short-term treatment services in less than half the areas.
- Over a third of carers reported having difficulties getting respite care.

Teamwork and strategy need further attention
- Only one-third of areas had jointly agreed assessment and care management procedures.
- Only a handful had compatible IT systems.
- A quarter lacked clear goals.

Some areas have good mental health services for older people in place, but many do not. The *National Service Framework for Older People* provides a framework for all agencies to improve their services to the standards of the best. All areas should strive to improve services for some of the most vulnerable people in society.
- The above article is from the February 2002 update of the report *Forget Me Not* published by the Audit Commission. © *Audit Commission February 2002*

Elderly suffer 'patchy' mental health services

ental health services for older people are patchy, with specialist teams unavailable to help elderly patients in some areas of England, the government's public spending watchdog said today.

A report from the audit commission – *Forget Me Not 2002* – found that less than half of the areas examined had fully available specialist mental health teams for the elderly.

More than a third of GPs felt they did not have ready access to specialist advice and it was not available in 40% of areas. Less than half of the GPs questioned felt they had had sufficient training to tackle dementia.

Commission controller Sir Andrew Foster said: 'In our later years, many of us are vulnerable to mental health problems such as Alzheimer's disease and other forms of dementia. It's at this point that we need lots of support and good quality care. However, our update shows clearly this is not happening everywhere.

'Things need to change and that change needs to happen quickly. People over 85 are the fastest-growing age group in the country, so demands on mental health services from older people are not going to let up.'

The report says less than 50% of all specialist day hospitals provide consistent access to services, and the availability of planned respite care varies considerably across the country. On average less than two-thirds of carers said they could get help to give them a break.

There were warnings from social services staff that some GPs were delaying the identification of mental health problems in older people, leaving situations to reach crisis point before specialist services were alerted.

The audit commission said GP practices must make increased efforts to diagnose dementia and depression in elderly people.

It said health authorities, councils and trusts providing mental health services must work together to strengthen and improve services for some of the most vulnerable people in society.

The report adds that local mental health professionals need to offer more guidance, training and support to GPs and primary care staff in the management of dementia and depression.

© *Guardian Newspapers Limited 2002*

Free personal care for elderly backed in poll

Pensioners forced to sell homes to pay for basic needs

By Rebecca Allison

When Mary Johnson's mother fell ill she was forced to pay for her sick husband to go into a nursing home so that she could travel across the country to help. When her mother died a few months later, she had to pay for him to be looked after again, so that she could attend the funeral.

The former maths teacher's case is typical according to charities. The issue of free care for the elderly came top of the viewers' poll on the BBC's NHS day series of programmes on Wednesday with 150,000 votes – far more than other health service priorities.

Mrs Johnson, 71, who has been the full-time carer for her husband Tony since he had a stroke in 1987, could not be in two places at once and there was no prospect of any free help. 'I was keeping them both outside of NHS care, outside hospital and I was, in effect, coping alone. I need more help, but we simply can't afford it,' she said.

The Johnsons are among thousands of elderly people in England and Wales who are not being provided with the state-funded long-term help they need. At least one in three women, and one in five men, need some care during retirement, in their own home or in a residential or nursing home. This can often mean large bills, with some pensioners being forced to sell their homes to meet costs.

Earlier this month, the Scottish parliament passed a bill enshrining free personal care for the elderly. But despite calls for similar provision south of the border, Tony Blair has repeatedly rejected such a move. Reacting to the BBC's poll he said: 'It would cost just over £1bn to do that. We are spending that £1bn differently.'

The NHS pays only for what is deemed to be nursing care. The bill for social or personal care, such as help with eating or washing, goes to social services and is means-tested.

The cut-off point of £18,000 for allowable savings is low enough that owning a house almost always rules out the right to free personal care.

A spokeswoman for the Right To Care Campaign said it was unfair that people at home or in residential and nursing homes were made to pay for the same basic care that would be free if they were in hospital.

'We are talking about care that people can't do without, like being fed, getting dressed and going to the toilet. It should not be the case that people at that stage of their lives, when they are vulnerable and need intensive care, should have to struggle just to survive and face losing their homes.'

Some elderly people have tried to avoid having to sell up to pay care bills by passing their house on to descendants. But if this is done within six months of needing care, the local authority can bill the new owners.

The Johnsons have yet to cross that bridge. The couple had more than £18,000 savings which disqualified them from free home care but they have so far avoided large bills because Mrs Johnson manages to cope with the minimum of outside help.

Mr Johnson, 72, was left unable to speak, read or write and paralysed down his right-hand side after his stroke and needs constant care.

As it is, they can just afford to pay £5.25 an hour for basic help from a council home care service representative who visits their home in Bourton, near Bristol, for four hours a week.

The case comes as no surprise to Help the Aged, who have helped spearhead the campaign for free personal care.

'As Scotland legislates for free personal care, the government's unfair and unworkable system of trying to distinguish free "nursing" care from means-tested "personal" care will prove itself to be untenable both in principle and in practice,' Tessa Harding, head of policy, said.

ADDITIONAL RESOURCES

You might like to contact the following organisations for further information. Due to the increasing cost of postage, many organisations cannot respond to enquiries unless they receive a stamped, addressed envelope.

Age Concern England
Astral House, 1268 London Road
London, SW16 4ER
Tel: 020 8765 7200
Fax: 020 8765 7211
E-mail: ace@ace.org.uk
Web site: www.ageconcern.org.uk
Age Concern co-ordinates a number of initiatives which promote healthier lifestyles, and provide older people with opportunities to give the experience of a lifetime back to their communities.

Alzheimer's Society
Gordon House, 10 Greencoat Place, London, SW1P 1PH
Tel: 020 7306 0606
Fax: 020 7306 0808
E-mail: enquiries@alzheimers.org.uk
Web site: www.alzheimers.org.uk
The UK's leading care and research charity for people with all forms of dementia and their carers. Their helpline: 0845 300 0336, 8am-6pm Monday to Friday, offers advice and support.

ARP/050 – The Association of Retired and Persons Over 50
Windsor House, 1270 London Road, London, SW16 4DH
Tel: 020 7828 0500
Fax: 020 7233 7132
E-mail: info@arp.org.uk
Web site: www.arp050.org.uk
Works to change the attitude towards age of individuals and society as a whole so as to enhance the quality of life for the over-50s, both present and future.

Campaign Against Age Discrimination in Employment (CAADE)
395 Barlow Road
Altrincham, WA14 5HW
Tel: 0845 345 8654
E-mail: caade@caade.net
Web site: www.caade.net
CAADE was formed to fight for the rights of older workers, particularly in the area of 'age discrimination in employment'.

Counsel and Care
Twyman House, 16 Bonny Street
London, NW1 9PG
Tel: 020 7241 8555
E-mail:
advice@counselandcare.org.uk
Web site:
www.counselandcare.org.uk
Counsel and Care's vision is for a society where older people are valued and respected, where they have choice and control over their lives and when they need help.

Economic and Social Research Council
Polaris House, North Star Avenue
Swindon, SN2 1UJ
Tel: 01793 413000
Fax: 01793 413130
E-mail: exrel@esrc.ac.uk
Web site: www.esrc.ac.uk
The ESRC is the UK's largest independent funding agency for research and postgraduate training into social and economic issues.

Help the Aged
207-221 Pentonville Road
London, N1 9UZ
Tel: 020 7278 1114
Fax: 020 7278 1116
E-mail: info@helptheaged.org.uk
Web site: www.helptheaged.org.uk
Aims to improve the quality of life for elderly people in the UK, particularly those who are frail, isolated or poor. Publishes useful factsheets and leaflets.

HelpAge International (HAI)
PO Box 32832
London, N1 9ZN
Tel: 020 7278 7778
Fax: 020 7843 1840
E-mail: hai@helpage.org
Web site: www.helpage.org
HelpAge International is a global network of not-for-profit organisations working with and for disadvantaged older people worldwide to achieve a lasting improvement in the quality of their lives. There are over 50 member organisations throughout the world.

Research into Ageing
PO Box 32833
London, N1 9ZQ
Tel: 020 7843 1550
E-mail: ria@ageing.co.uk
Web site: www.ageing.org
Please note that Research into Ageing does not have the resources to deal with individual enquiries. Teachers wanting copies of their free leaflets need to send an sae with their requests.

The Employers' Forum on Age
Astral House, 1268 London Road
London, SW16 4ER
Tel: 020 8765 7597
Fax: 020 8765 7374
E-mail: efa@ace.org.uk
Web site: www.efa-agediversity.org.uk
The Employers' Forum on Age is a network created by employers for employers. It is the first ever employer-led initiative that confronts the changes needed to achieve the business benefit of a mixed-age workforce.

The Work Foundation (formerly The Industrial Society)
Customer Centre
Quadrant Court
49 Calthorpe Road
Edgbaston, Birmingham, B15 1TH
Tel: 0870 165 6700
Fax: 0870 165 6701
E-mail: customercentre@thework
foundation.com
Web site:
www.theworkfoundation.com

Third Age Employment Network
207-221 Pentonville Road
London, N1 9UZ
Tel: 020 7843 1590
E-mail: taen@helptheaged.org.uk
Web site: www.taen.org.uk
The Third Age Employment Network aims to represent the interests of all mature people who want to continue training and working, so that they have the opportunities to use their skills and experience in the economy.

INDEX

ACKNOWLEDGEMENTS

The publisher is grateful for permission to reproduce the following material.

While every care has been taken to trace and acknowledge copyright, the publisher tenders its apology for any accidental infringement or where copyright has proved untraceable. The publisher would be pleased to come to a suitable arrangement in any such case with the rightful owner.

Chapter One: Ageing Trends

Older people in the United Kingdom, © 2002 Age Concern England, *Health life expectancy*, © World Health Organisation (WHO), *Older people in Britain*, © Counsel and Care, *The ageing of the world's population*, © United Nations Populations Division, (United Nations, New York 2002), *Population ageing*, © United Nations Populations Division, Population Ageing 2002 (United Nations, New York 2002), *Myths and conceptions*, © HelpAge International, *How men in the south live longer*, © The Daily Mail, March 2001, *An ageing world*, © HelpAge International, *Elderly people living alone*, © Crown copyright is reproduced with the permission of the Controller of Her Majesty's Stationery Office, *Fit and fifty?*, © Economic and Social Research Council (ESRC), *Over-50s statistics*, © The Association of Retired and Persons Over 50, *How the over-60s are taking over the world*, © The Daily Mail, April 2002, *Ageing issues*, © 2002 Age Concern England, *Seniors in the medias*, © The Association of Retired and Persons Over 50, *How pensioners are treated in the UK and in Europe*, © Graphical Paper Media Union (GPMU).

Chapter Two: Ageism in the Workplace

Age discrimination, © The Work Foundation, *Age – the issues for today's workplace*, © The Employers' Forum on Age, *Now you're over the hill at 42*, © Guardian Newspapers Limited 2002, *Useful facts and figures*, © The Employers' Forum on Age, *Key facts on age diversity and employment*, © Third Age Employment Network, *Employment status by age*, © Chartered Institute of Personnel and Development (CIPD), *Learning to value experience*, © Guardian Newspapers Limited 2002, *£31 billion per year*, ©

The Employers' Forum on Age, *Experience of age discrimination*, © Third Age Employment Network, *Redundancies*, © Chartered Institute of Personnel and Development (CIPD), *The worldwide picture*, © Campaign Against Age Discrimination in Employment (CAADE), *Record number of businesses started by over-50s*, © Barclays Group, *Experience necessary*, © The Work Foundation, *Add seven years to your working life*, © Guardian Newspapers Limited 2002, *The statistical timebombs*, © Campaign Against Age Discrimination in Employment (CAADE), *Pension age 'must rise to 67 for all'*, © Guardian Newspapers Limited 2002, *Age Concern highlights pension anxiety*, © Guardian Newspapers Limited 2002.

Chapter Three: Ageing and Health

Old and on the scrapheap, © Help the Aged, *Ageing*, © Research into Ageing, *Longstanding conditions*, © Crown copyright is reproduced with the permission of the Controller of Her Majesty's Stationery Office, *Health crisis looms as life expectancy soars*, © Guardian Newspapers Limited 2002, *Elderly 'missing out on basic care'*, © Guardian Newspapers Limited 2002, *Healthy old age is myth for many*, © MORI (Market & Opinion Research International Limited), *Turning your back on us*, © 2002 Age Concern England, *Dementia*, © Alzheimer's Society, *Alzheimer's*, © Alzheimer's Society, *Alzheimer's cases in UK 'will double in 40 years'*, © The Daily Mail, April 2002, *Forget me not 2002*, © Audit Commission, February 2002, *Elderly suffer 'patchy' mental health services*, © Guardian Newspapers Limited 2002, *Free personal care for elderly backed in poll*, © Guardian Newspapers Limited 2002.

Photographs and illustrations:

Pages 1, 8, 19, 24, 34, 37, 40: Simon Kneebone; pages 5, 20, 27: Bev Aisbett; pages 11, 13, 31: Fiona Katauskas; pages 23, 26, 32: Pumpkin House.

Craig Donnellan
Cambridge
September, 2002